UNMASKING DARKNESS

Your Power to Overcome Demonic Warfare

DR. STEPHEN R BUCHANAN

Unmasking Darkness
Your Power to Overcome Demonic Warfare
© 2022 by Dr. Stephen R. Buchanan

All rights reserved solely by the author. The author guarantees all contents are original and do not infringe upon the legal rights of any other person or work. No part of this book may be reproduced in any form without the permission of the author. The views expressed in this book are not necessarily those of the publisher.

Scriptures marked NKJV are taken from the NEW KING JAMES VERSION (NKJV): Scripture taken from the NEW KING JAMES VERSION®. Copyright© 1982 by Thomas Nelson, Inc. Used by permission. All rights reserved.

Scriptures marked NIV are taken from the NEW INTERNATIONAL VERSION (NIV): Scripture taken from THE HOLY BIBLE, NEW INTERNATIONAL VERSION ®. Copyright© 1973, 1978, 1984, 2011 by Biblica, Inc.TM. Used by permission of Zondervan

Printed in the United States of America.
ISBN-13: 978-1-7373939-0-0

Cover design: Quezart, Inc

MEG Publishing
Florida, U.S.A

DEDICATED TO THE BODY OF CHRIST

TABLE OF CONTENT

Introduction	1
Chapter 1 Innocence Shattered	5
Chapter 2 Too Close For Comfort	8
Chapter 3 Into The Ring Of Fire	11
Chapter 4 Stepping Into The Light	17
Chapter 5 Occult And The Bible	27
Chapter 6 Demon Possession	32
Chapter 7 The Source Of Dark Power	41
Chapter 8 Spiritual Warfare	52
Chapter 9 Enemy Number 1 - Principalities	56
Chapter 10 Enemy Number 2 - Powers	70
Chapter 11 Enemy Number 3 - Rulers Of Darkness	73
Chapter 12 Enemy Number 4 - Spiritual Wickedness In High Places	76
Chapter 13 The Armor Of God	81
Chapter 14 The Belt Of Truth	83
Chapter 15 The Shoe – Gospel Of Peace	94
Chapter 16 The Shield Of Faith	98
Chapter 17 The Helmet Of Salvation	103

Chapter 18 Sword Of The Spirit	108
Chapter 19 God Speaks	111
Chapter 20 Prayer	114
Chapter 21 The Destiny Of Demons	124
Chapter 22 Go In Confidence	127

INTRODUCTION

The experiences you are about to read in this book are experiences I have never shared before. I find it necessary to share them now since there are many believers, unknowingly get involve with demonic activities. They do so, not understanding the severe spiritual consequences of their actions. The impact of these demonic interactions can last for many generations and come with a high price.

I believe that God allowed these experiences to occur in preparation for the assignment that was on my life. Years later in my deliverance ministry, I have confronted and cast out demons all around the USA, and the Caribbean. I have witnessed the spitting, snarls, and contortions of human bodies, as people manifested demonic possessions. I have been aware of demons and their powerful works ranging from: freeing the guilty criminal, giving wealth and fame to those willing to trade their souls for it, imposing sickness and diseases, to destroying families and relationships.

As I study the scriptures, I have come to realize that there is nothing new concerning demonic activities on the earth. God made it very clear in His Word, what is the source of evil and the nature of our spiritual warfare. There is no denying the presence of the power of demonic forces, but I have seen throughout scripture that there is a greater power at work – God Almighty. We must understand the power of God that is at work within us and how we have been positioned to operate in victory over our enemy.

We are in a season now more than ever, when Christians need to understand spiritual warfare. The intention of this book is to take you to a practical place as it relates to spiritual warfare. Life is full of seasons, and you have an enemy who will press into you and your family at times with all intentions to kill steal and destroy. There are going to be times in your life where it feels like God has forgotten you. God never abandons his children but we are call to resist the devil and he will flee. This book will be an essential handbook for all believers to gain greater understanding of demonic activities and the day to day impact of these spiritual beings on our daily lives.

"For the weapons of our warfare are not carnal, but mighty through God to the pulling down of strong holds;) 5 Casting down imaginations, and every high thing that exalteth itself against the knowledge of God, and bringing into captivity every thought to the obedience of Christ;

2 Corinthians 10:4-5 KjV

It is important to understand spiritual warfare so, you can be prepared to handle the attacks and deprivation that our enemy, the devil will bring upon us and our family members.

CHAPTER 1

INNOCENCE SHATTERED

And this is the condemnation, that the light has come into the world, and men loved darkness rather than light, because their deeds were evil. For everyone practicing evil hates the light and does not come to the light, lest his deeds should be exposed.

John 3:19-20

It was a sleepy, quiet, fishing village nestled in a remote part of the island. Everyone seem like we were a part of a tribal commune. We were all relatives in one way or another. All of the children rustled from house to house, playing marbles, handball, and other games we created on the spot for fun. Ladies sat in the shade of a Lignum Vitae tree washing pans of clothing with bare hands. It seem like quite a task but I loved to see the clothing which hung from lines that stretched from tree to tree fluttering in the gentle sea breeze.

Men in the meantime spent their days working on building fishing traps made from sticks and a special fishing wire. Each one would stop by to give a helping hand to each other throughout the day. Thinking about my childhood village brings back fun memories. So, what could ever possibly be wrong in this homely place? It would not take me long, even at a tender age to realize that the village was not that innocent at all and luring beneath it quaint family facade evil lurks. Like the rest of the world, I would soon come to know that our village was filled with greed, envy, and jealousy. It would be in this context that I was about to encounter the dark world of witchcraft known to the locals as Obeah.

Some people were very open in their practice of Obeah while others were subtle in their intent. Some practice for evil while others claim to practice for self-help. I recall waking up one morning and seeing a pole raised across the street with a red flag fluttering in the soft sea breeze. A closer look revealed that there was a frog hanging from it by its hind leg just beneath the flag. My young innocent mind wondered what that sighting was all about. It seems cruel to me and certainly there was nothing pleasant about it. Other neighbors stared fearfully at this symbol and drifted to the next side of the road as they hurriedly passed by it. "What was that?" I thought, but when I dared to ask, I was told to be quiet and mind my own business. "Shush!" I was told with a tone that, even as a child I knew I was protected from something sinister, something that drove fear in people hearts. My young inquisitive mind still needed answers; why would those who seemed to be the most materially comfortable create such strange sightings in the community? Yes, the 'flag and frog flying' neighbor had the largest home, the longest boat, and the only car in our village.

The primary source of income was fishing, and it was customary for the men to go only once per week. Other nights of the week they gathered underneath one of the three streetlamps that lit the village's only street. With cigarettes stuck in the right corners of their lips and a small cup of white rum a favorite alcoholic beverage at their ankles, they would talk about the people in the village. "He has a good Obeah man", one said referring to my neighbor as he pulled on his cigarette and waited for his turn in a game of dominoes. Another acknowledged that based on the results - of material success our flag flying villager had an effective witch. "For sure" he said and continue after a brief pause. "I think he is in St Thomas" referring to the eastern area of the island. "Okay," I whispered to myself, now making sense of the flag and the frog.

CHAPTER 2

TOO CLOSE FOR COMFORT

It was about 3:00 am one morning, and I had a sleepover at a relative's house (not uncommon since the whole village is family). This relative was doing very well and his children were also doing extremely well. After all, they owned a color TV (a novelty at the time), drove, and lived in a nicer house than others in the village. They were a church-going family; every Sunday he would commute to church with his family. I had heard of God's immense goodness and so I was sure that the Lord had just really helped this family, but the purity and innocence of my childish expectation was about to be shocked.

I was not supposed to be awake; and I thought, whoever is moving about the house should be asleep too unless they meant to be up for a reason. It felt creepy and I must admit, I was petrified; 'What was happening?' I thought to myself as I peeked from beneath the sheets, pretending to be asleep. The image of my relative came into view. "Should I pretend to be snoring to let him think I am asleep?" I thought, but I could not hold my breath as it seemed as if the oxygen had been sucked out of the room.

"It's his house, he has the right to walk around in it but what is he doing?" I wondered, my heart racing. I fixed my eyes to watch, squinting as hard as I could so as not to miss any detail.

He quietly walked through the room with a small vial in his hand, and I watched as he sprinkled its content throughout the room and other parts of the house. I did not mention this incident to anyone, not even my father; after all, I knew he would say, "Shush!"

I was old enough to figure out what I was seeing. I learned that there are two sides to witchcraft practices; on the one hand, evil is invoked, and the other hand people seek protection from others folks harmful intent. Either way, they are both dancing with the devil. Sadly, on that night, my image of this wholesome, god-fearing family was shattered.

Reflecting on this instance brings Matthew 22: 27-28 to mind,

> *"Woe to you, teachers of the law and Pharisees, you hypocrites! You are like whitewashed tombs, which look beautiful on the outside but on the inside are full of the bones of the dead and everything unclean. In the same way, you appear to people as righteous on the outside, but you are full of hypocrisy and wickedness on the inside."*

How many times do we appear to be one thing on the outside for people to see, but we are entirely different on the inside? It is so sad that many Christians put on a façade for people to see and think that they are fully committed to following the precepts of God.

It is easy to make something look clean on the outside, while still being dirty on the inside. Many people appear to be very well put together and "clean" but many times that is not the true picture. It's like having a clean and well-maintained lawn, but inside the house is filthy and messy. I've lived long enough to know that people's lives can look very good on the outside – they dress nicely, they smile, give generously, go to church, volunteer, and do all manner of good, yet on the inside they are filthy.

It is important that we take care of our insides as well. Just as we wash our bodies to keep clean on the outside, so should we take care of our inner being – our hearts and minds must be washed clean by God's word. (Ephesians 5:26)

CHAPTER 3

INTO THE RING OF FIRE

Fast forward a couple of years after the incident at my relative's home. Now as a teenager I was about to embark on a very important trip. I had done well in school and had just received a full scholarship to college. Naturally, like any caring and concerned parent in a spiritually hostile community, they were determined that I have a promising future, not deterred by the evil of jealousy that occurred in our village. Their mission, to protect me from any such evil (Obeah spells) by those who would be envious of the fact that I was award this scholastic achievement, took us on a road trip. I went along willingly. After all, I had seen people bewitched in the village - people who lost their minds and lived in caves snarling and acting like animals, and that was before I even saw it in the Bible. These were powerful forces at work.

After a few hours of winding through hilly terrains, we pulled up in a yard with a small chapel-like building. People were walking with special head wrappings, and from seeing similar people on television and hearing stories, I quickly identified them as spiritualists. These were people who practiced the spiritual ritual traditions brought over to the Caribbean by the African slaves, fused with some elements of Christianity. I could hear the sound of drums beating, and the echoes which rattled back from the alluring hills surrounding the yard added to the mystic grandeur of this (strange) place. Chants accompanied the rhythm, and as I approached, there was a group of drummers and singers dressed in white tunics and interesting head wraps. It was all so very mystical, and to a 13-year-old boy, it was like going to Disney for the first time.

After paying a fee or a "gift" - as they preferred to call it - at the entrance, we sat on wooden benches waiting to be seen. Many people were waiting to be seen, each waiting anxiously to be called next. The wait was long, and as I sat there listening to the rhythms of the drums, I perused my surroundings. If it were nowadays, I would be the kid that sat there on the phone or tablet or any other smart device until the battery ran out, but no, instead, I was mesmerized by the floor of this little chapel-like building. All materials used for its construction were harnessed from its surroundings. In the front was a podium which was raised by a tree trunk and deck on top by pieces of boards that looked like refuse from a construction site.

The building had window ways but no windows. What would happen if it rained? I thought to myself.

After several hours of waiting, or should I say all day waiting, it was now dusk, and finally, it was my turn to be seen by the chief spiritualist - a woman they called "Mother." We went down to where a little pool was dug in the ground, just large enough to be some kind of water catchment for rituals. I was spun around numerous times while water from the pool was poured around my feet. How ridiculous is this? I thought to myself, what can this water really do to protect me? I would never know if it mattered or what else came with it since I did go to school successfully, and here I am today, telling this story, still in my right mind. I was bewildered by how many people participated in these practices daily.

In my next recollection, I was a mere observer but close enough to the insider. This event I would only fully understand as I studied the Bible later in life. A good friend of mine (let's call her Urlia) was relating to me how she was owed money by a business acquaintance who had refused to pay. "I want my money back!" she said angrily, "and I am going to make him pay!" She and I were close friends, so she did not mind expressing herself, "when I finish with him, he will bring it quickly!" she continued. "What are you going to do?" I asked. "Just come with me," she said adamantly. So, I went for the ride.

First, we stopped to pick a young goat, which she had bought from a local herdsman. The poor goat was tied up and put inside the trunk of the car. The scared animal's bellows could be heard from behind the car seat. This was such cruelty but paled in comparison to what this little guy would face in an hour. We drove to a village where a witch doctor practiced. When we pulled up to the house, the first thing I noticed was flying flags. "O, Lord!" I thought to myself, red flags! This image brought back memories from my childhood, where I'd seen the flag and frog hanging. We alighted from the car and were greeted by a lanky gentleman wearing khaki pants and a plaid shirt. Judging by how excited they were to see each other; my guess was that this was not Urlia's first time here. I was told to sit on the veranda where chairs were provided while they walked away, whispering as they discussed the mission. Curious about my environment, I searched around with investigative eyes. This place was different; there was no singing or drumming, no chapel, just an eerie silence.

It was dusk, and since my movement was limited, I could only investigate my immediate surroundings. I looked through the window just behind my chair. Inside the room was a small table with burning candles – red and white ones. The yard was swept clean, maybe by the man I met earlier, and flowering plants lined the fence. We had to wait for nightfall to come as this ritual required the cover of darkness. As night fell, there was a grinding sound somewhere in the back. It's a sound I recognized growing up in a fishing and farming village; it was the sound of a sharpening file against the blade of a machete.

Finally, the witch (Obeah woman) came out; she was a very plump figured woman in her late fifties or early sixties. She was dressed in her ritual clothes – a white tunic and a red and yellow turban on her head with a red band tied around her waist which seemed more like under her bosom since she had a large stomach. She immediately asked who I was and if I was trustworthy, and Urlia quickly assured her that I was a very good friend and could be trusted. I really wanted to see this ritual, but I was not allowed to go to the back with them, where the blood sacrifice was about to occur. I could, however, hear the poor animal we had brought with us; he was struggling, wrestling as they constrained him. The poor goat would soon lose the battle. You could hear its piercing screams as the machete cut through his throat.

I knew the sound, as we've slaughtered goats in my village for special celebrations such as weddings and Christmas. As the goat's whimper died out, I knew he was being offered up in the ritual sacrifice. Its gut- wrenching cry as the blade cut through its throat was unforgettable. After all, we had no meat going back with us; this was different; this was not for food. Although I couldn't help thinking that the Obeah woman would eat all that good meat, this was a demonic ritual. Maybe that explains her weight. This ritual of offering animals is as old as time itself and is alluded to in the book of Deuteronomy 26:14.

> *I have not eaten any of the sacred portions while I was in mourning, nor have I removed any of it. At the same time, I was unclean, nor have I offered any of it to the dead.*

CHAPTER 4

STEPPING INTO THE LIGHT

My church upbringing was primarily conservative, growing up predominantly in the United Christian Brethren denomination. Here, little was ever mentioned about demons. There were no overt expressions of the Holy Spirit as seen in Pentecostal churches, no speaking in tongues, no falling down, no screaming, or anything of that sort. For that reason, I was not exposed to many spiritual expressions in human beings. I wasn't privy to watching television as a child because we didn't have one, and whenever we did get an opportunity to watch TV, it was a grainy display due to poor signal from the only TV station on the island. In those days, Christian TV was Billy Graham's crusades and Jimmy Swaggart's. Whenever I watched, I saw people with tears running down their faces from conviction; that was new and all so strange to me.

However, I had an interesting experience in prayer one Friday night as I received the baptism of the Holy Spirit. I had come to recognize what praying in tongues was and the biblical truth about it. This was never taught in our church. It really triggered my interest in the work of the Holy Spirit and His impact on us as Christians. It also led me inevitably to discover the Bible's teaching on the effects of the spiritual world on human beings.

Demons:

Several activities are identified in the Bible in which demons may be involved. Sometimes they are responsible for physical disease or mental suffering. While not all mental disorders are demonic in origin, some are. Demons are also credited with tempting people to engage in immoral practices. They are the originators and propagators of the false doctrines taught by heretical religious groups. The Bible also teaches that demons possessed some people. Demons are committed to evil, yet God will use them to accomplish His plan during the end times.

Demons unknowingly do the will of God. It must be frustrating to demons after they had accomplished some evil scheme to find out later that they were carrying out the will of God. Satan did not realize what God wanted to do in Job's life when he caused him physical suffering. Also, God used 'an evil spirit' to accomplish His will in the life of Saul, Israel's first king (1 Sam. 16:14). On another occasion, God used 'a lying spirit' to deceive the false prophets of an evil king (1 Kings

22:22, 23). At the end of the Great Tribulation, demons will be used by God to gather the nations of the world to the battlefields of Armageddon (Rev. 9:16). God can use even demons to accomplish His will.

There are many reasons why a person may experience physical illness. Sometimes it is the result of God's judgment for sin (1 Cor. 11:30). On other occasions, the same sickness may come as a result of breaking some health law and exposing oneself to germs or viruses. It may come from God as His means of ending a person's life naturally. On other occasions, demons may be the reason a person experiences physical suffering.

Several specific physical afflictions are attributed to demons in the Bible. Jesus cast a demon out of a dumb man who immediately began to speak (Matt. 9:32, 33). On another occasion, a blind man began to see when the demon went out of him (Matt. 12:22). Job was afflicted physically with boils covering his body, the result of satanic activity (Job 2:1-10). Demons may have been the messengers that carried out Satan's commands to smite Job. Of course, afflictions are not always symptoms of demon activity, but demons are capable of and do occasionally cause physical pain and suffering.

Various forms of mental diseases can also be attributed to demons. In at least two cases of demon possession treated by Jesus during his ministry, the demons had affected the minds of the victims to cause abnormal behavior. One man lived among tombs, a practice considered unclean during this time, and created a disturbance day and night (Mark 5:4, 5).

A young boy possessed with a demon involuntarily went into an apparent convulsion when he encountered the presence of Jesus (Luke 9:37-42). In both instances, the victims engaged in some form of self-destruction and physical mutilation of the body. After the demon was cast out of the person, the apparent mental problem disappeared. I have seen firsthand this demonic mental torment. There was a brilliant young man in my village that was a few years older than I; I remember him as a well-dressed, well- spoken, well-read, and handsome by all standards. He went crazy overnight, literally. What made this so intriguing and mysterious was that he immediately removed himself from his house, entered into a rock cave behind the family's home, and began living like an animal. He lived in that dark cave surrounded by only the animals that called it their home for as long as my memory serves me. No one had seen this before, and everybody knew something spiritual had happened, but the church had no guts to confront that demon, and frankly, neither did I.

For the Christian, our final moral code of ethics is the Bible. Those who oppose God will also oppose the morality of the Bible. Demons are instrumental in leading both the saved and unsaved into moral compromise. One of the often-used names for demons in the Bible is 'unclean spirit,' an appropriate name, as they tarnish everything they influence. When Israel left Egypt, God gave them the land of Canaan. One of the reasons God wanted them in a separate land was that the heathen nations had given themselves over to unclean spirits and had become corrupted.

> *When you enter the land the Lord your God is giving you, do not learn to imitate the detestable ways of the nations there. Let no one be found among you who sacrifices their son or daughter in the fire, who practices divination or sorcery, interprets omens, engages in witchcraft, or casts spells, or who is a medium or spiritist or who consults the dead. Anyone who does these things is detestable to the Lord; the Lord, your God, will drive out those nations before you because of these same detestable practices. You must be blameless before the Lord your God.*
>
> **Deut. 18: 9-13**

Paul discussed one main work of demons when he warned young Timothy of conditions in the latter times. "Now the Spirit expressly says that in latter times some will depart from the faith by devoting themselves to deceitful spirits and teachings of demons." 1Timothy 4:1.

Demons are the source of many organized doctrines of the false cults. Even in the early church, there were false apostles. We read in Rev. 2:2, where it says, *"I know your deeds, your hard work, and your perseverance. I know that you cannot tolerate wicked people, that you have tested those who claim to be apostles but are not, and have found them false."* There were also false doctrines -- *"Nevertheless, I have a few things against you: There are some among you who hold to the teaching of Balaam, who taught Balak to entice the Israelites to sin so that they ate food sacrificed to idols and committed sexual immorality." (Rev. 2:14)*; and all of these had to be opposed. The church needs to better understand demonic works around us, so as to be prepared to counter them. Battling demonic forces is not an option for the army of God. Preparation must begin with our purity.

The Bible teaches about the coming of an antichrist during the Great Tribulation but, by the end of the first century, John wrote, *"Dear children, this is the last hour, and as you have heard that the antichrist is coming, even now many antichrists have come. This is how we know it is the last hour." (1 John 2:18)*. The word 'anti' has a twofold designation; first, it meant 'against' Christ, but the secondary meaning was the most evident; it meant "in substitution for," or "instead of," Christ. The existence of 'antichrist' leaders throughout the church age is the result of demon activity. Their main activity is to foster a 'substitute religion' in place of Christ and his doctrine.

Therefore, it is clearly demonic even when we seek spiritual involvement not to harm but to protect other sources. Many Christians have found themselves in these practices, and most cease to understand the risk of losing their salvation. One of the chief difficulties of living for God today is not the social pressures or inconvenience of life; it is the spiritual battle we are engaged in. Our enemies are demons. Paul observed, "For we do not wrestle against flesh and blood, but against the rulers, against the authorities, against the cosmic powers over this present darkness, against the spiritual forces of evil in the heavenly places." (Eph. 6:12). The phrase "the rulers, against the authorities, against the cosmic powers over this present darkness, against the spiritual forces of evil" refers to demons and their activities.

Part of the work of demons, particularly related to the Christian life, is doing battle with Christians on the spiritual level. This condition is the reason behind the apostolic imperative, "Put on the whole armor of God that you may be able to stand against the schemes of the devil." (Eph. 6:11). Without spiritual help from God, the Christian is unable to win the battle against demons. In rare instances, the Bible mentions demons by name. These demons had such an impact on the lives of believers that their presence warranted mention by the writers of the Scripture.

Molech:

Although the scriptures never explicitly refer to Molech as a demon, the worship of Molech was a recurring problem for Israel throughout the Old Testament. The origin of Molech worship is unclear. Scholars believe that Molech worship came to the region of Canaan with the Phoenicians.

> *You shall not give any of your children to offer them to Molech, and so profane the name of your God: I am the Lord.*
>
> **Leviticus 18:21**

Then Solomon built a high place for Chemosh, the abomination of Moab, and for Molech, the abomination of the Ammonites, on the mountain east of Jerusalem (1 Kings 11:7). One of the most documented practices of Molech worship was that of human sacrifice. Molech worship reached its peak during the reign of Solomon and would not be abolished until the time of captivity in Babylon.

Legion:

Demons in the Bible often congregate together, and one example is Legion. When Jesus arrived at the country of the Gerasenes, He encountered a possessed man outside the city in a cemetery. We read about this in Mark 5:2-10

> When Jesus got out of the boat, a man with an impure spirit came from the tombs to meet him. 3 This man lived in the tombs, and no one could bind him anymore, not even with a chain. 4 For he had often been chained hand and foot, but he tore the chains apart and broke the irons on his feet. No one was strong enough to subdue him. 5 Night and day among the tombs and in the hills, he would cry out and cut himself with stones. 6 When he saw Jesus from a distance, he ran and fell on his knees in front of him. 7 He shouted at the top of his voice, "What do you want with me, Jesus, Son of the Most High God? In God's name, don't torture me!" 8 For Jesus had said to him, "Come out of this man, you impure spirit!" 9 Then Jesus asked him, "What is your name?" "My name is Legion," he replied, "for we are many." 10 And he begged Jesus again and again not to send them out of the area.

The man was not only considered a menace, but he had such great strength that he could not be contained. When Jesus spoke to the man, the Demons within him referred to themselves as Legion, for there was not one demon but many.

Abaddon/Apollyon:

One of the most frightening examples of demons mentioned in the Bible is Abaddon. John describes Abaddon during the 'Seven Trumpets' prophecy. *They had as king over them the angel of the Abyss, whose name in Hebrew is Abaddon and in Greek is Apollyon (that is, Destroyer),* (Revelation 9:11).

When the fifth trumpet is blown, the 'abyss' will open, and demonic locusts will be released to torture those who have not received God's seal. Their leader will be Abaddon, one of Satan's underlings and leader of the 'abyss.' Abaddon will have a simple mission – inflicting pain and suffering on those who have not responded to God and accepted Jesus Christ as their savior.

CHAPTER 5

OCCULT AND THE BIBLE

Satan is worshipped in several ways through the occults, some of these ways are:

Divination:

Divination was one of the specific practices named by Moses in his prohibition on occult worship. "Let no one be found among you who sacrifices their son or daughter in the fire, who practices divination or sorcery, interprets omens, engages in witchcraft" Deut. 18:10.

Oftentimes this practice included the killing of a chicken or some small animal, and on occasions to observe its liver to determine the state of affairs and direction of the immediate future. This is likened to modern-day palm reading, tarot cards, or crystal balls. "For the king of Babylon will stop at the fork in the road, at the junction of the two roads, to seek an omen: He will cast lots with arrows, he will consult his idols, he will examine the liver." Ezek. 21:21. Divination is an illegitimate means of determining the will of God. The Christian desiring to know the will of God should consult the Scriptures, not the stars. "Your word is a lamp for my feet and a light on my path." Ps. 119:105

Necromancy:

Necromancy is another occult practice that God banned. It is an effort to communicate with and interrogate the dead. Since the Bible teaches the dead are unable to communicate with the living, it only stands to reason that those who claim to have this ability are lying or are themselves deceived. We are reminded of this in: Luke 16:27-31

> *"He answered, 'Then I beg you, father, send Lazarus to my family, for I have five brothers. Let him warn them so that they will not also come to this place of torment.' Abraham replied, 'They have Moses and the Prophets; let them listen to them.' 'No, Father Abraham,' he said, 'but if someone from the dead goes to them, they will repent.' He said to him, 'If they do not listen to Moses and the Prophets, they will not be convinced even if someone rises from the dead.'"*

We have seen television shows dedicated to this practice. We have even seen its promotion by famous influencers such as

Oprah Winfrey on her show. In either case, the necromancer was considered an abomination unto the Lord. *Deut. 18:11-12* *"...or casts spells, or who is a medium or spiritist or who consults the dead. Anyone who does these things is detestable to the Lord; because of these same detestable practices, the Lord your God will drive out those nations before you."*

Magic:

The use of magic formulas and incantations was also forbidden. Today it is popular to distinguish between white and black magic, but leading biblical scholars agree that both forms of magic find their source and strength in demonic power. Those who practice magic are under certain limits as to what they can accomplish.

When the magicians, enchanters, astrologers, and diviners came, I told them the dream, but they could not interpret it for me. Daniel 4:7 Even when it appears that magicians can duplicate the power of God, they still fall short of what God can accomplish.

Exodus 7:11-12, "Pharaoh then summoned wise men and sorcerers, and the Egyptian magicians also did the same things by their secret arts: Each one threw down his staff, and it became a snake. But Aaron's staff swallowed up their staffs."

Sorcery:

Closely related to magic is sorcery. Magic usually relates to accomplishing specific acts-such as rods becoming serpents, whereas sorcery relates more closely with calling upon demons to create situations around people. Therefore, the enchanter or sorcerer uses incantations or omens. Their practices may have also included the use of mood-changing or mind-altering drugs. This has led some Bible scholars to denounce the use of such drugs because they are used as part of occult worship.

Witchcraft:

There are a growing number of people around the world today who call themselves witches. Witchcraft is directly opposed to God, as seen in *Deut. 18:10* "Let no one be found among you who sacrifices their son or daughter in the fire, who practices divination or sorcery, interprets omens, engages in witchcraft."

When Saul became the first king of Israel, one of his first acts was to ban the practice of witchcraft from the kingdom. 1 Sam. 28:9, "But the woman said to him, 'Surely you know what Saul has done. He has cut off the mediums and spiritists from the land. Why have you set a trap for my life to bring about my death?"

A witch makes use of magic and sorcery to accomplish the will of demons.

Astrology:

One of the oldest forms of the occult still practiced today is astrology. Contemporary astrology is a combination of what astrological cults practiced in Babylon, Egypt, and Canaan. In Canaan, astrology centered around the bull. The worship of the golden calf, child sacrifices to Molech, and Baal worship were all part of Canaanite astrology. The Old Testament is very clear to prohibit God's people from getting involved with these practices.

In Egypt, God challenged the astrological gods of Egypt by sending ten plagues that directly attacked the authority of those gods. The highest of the Egyptian gods was Ra, the sun god. God sent three days of darkness on the land. There is no God like Jehovah!

CHAPTER 6

DEMON POSSESSION

Demon possession or demon control is more than simply a carry-over of ancient superstitions. As we understand it, demon possession occurs when demons possess a person and control their mind or body. On many occasions, demon possession resulted in mental derangement. In most cases recorded in Scripture, the person possessed was clearly responsible for being possessed.

Understanding Demon Possession

There is much confusion about demon possession. Demon possession is the culmination of a deliberate rejection of God and a volitional acceptance of Satan and his demons. Every unclean life is vulnerable to demon possession, but actions and environments often encourage and invite them to participate in a person's life. As much as I am tempted to start making a list, it would be too exhaustive for this book. The general rule is anything or actions that are unclean will do.

Demon possession is the opposite of the filling of the Spirit. Just as Christians are more effective when filled with the Holy Spirit, so unbelievers have greater demonic power because of their demonic possession. The same word 'fill' is used of the Holy Spirit controlling in Ephesians 5:18 as Satan's control of Ananias and Sapphira in Acts 5. Demon possession and demon activities are more commonly recognized in third-world countries. However, there is increasing evidence of demonic activity in Western societies because of its waning Christian influence. As our nation turns from God and more people worship Satan and demons, there will be more evidence of demonic activities in our society.

I have had my share of direct encounters with demon-possessed people. There are three most memorable encounters/manifestations that never leave my mind. In the earlier years of my ministry, I traveled as an evangelist and psalmist. One trip took me to the British Virgin Islands. I began to pray for many during the service when Sarah (not her real name) began to convulse. It was clear that something unusual was happening. The prayer warriors around me intensified their war cry, and so did the physical expression of this poor soul. She was restrained by three strong men who notably had a hard time containing her strength. They brought her to me to address; after all, I was the guest preacher who's supposed to be powerful. I was familiar with seeing deliverance in action, but I'd never been required to do the job—this time, I had to confront it. The ball was in my court. I laid hands on her, and she collapsed to the floor. As I bent down to pray, she began throwing up and slimming. What followed was a sight I could only compare to a childhood memory of waking up to find our guard dog poisoned, lying dying. After a while, she came to rest, but she was not dead. She looked around the room strangely as if unaware of what had just taken place when she came to.

I visited the island two years later to minister at a different church, and just as I arrived and was heading to the hosting area for the guest preacher, a lady came towards me excited. "Do you remember me?" she asked. I tried to recall who she was, but nothing jogged my memory. Seeing that I did not recognize her, she continued, to my relief; I felt embarrassed that I didn't, and the look on her face said she thought I should. "I was the person who received deliverance from demons when you were here on the island two years ago," she said with that sweet musical Eastern Caribbean accent. I immediately remembered the incident, but she looked so amazing now, happy, refreshed, and renewed. Dressed in a beautiful modest dress, she swayed to and fro, hands animated as if dancing to a calypso rhythm as she told me a bit more about the joy of living in freedom. I wanted to listen more, but I had to leave. As I sat waiting to be called to the podium, my mind was in awe. I couldn't help reflecting on the miracle I'd just witnessed outside. I was just simply in awe of God's amazing power.

Somehow deliverance became a part of my work as I traveled. I remember I was hosting a special deliverance service at a church in Florida. I was in prayer and fasting for three days, and on the day of the service, I had spent all day locked in the church hall in prayer. That night we saw two mighty works of God over demons.

There was a lady who was brought to the meeting by her two daughters. She had been dumb for twenty-one years, with no medical explanation, I was told. She was about five feet two inches in height and overweight, dressed in black; her bloodshot eyes were more noticeable and almost scary. Was this a true deliverance request, or was it a demonic showdown? I was fearless; after all, I knew I was well prepared for spiritual warfare. Instead of laying hands on her, I began to address the Spirit, and it began to manifest itself - there slimming, vomiting, and making erratic movements. She was held securely by several people, who had come with her believing for a miracle, and in minutes she received her ability to speak again. What a joy! Following her deliverance, I saw relief, joy, and peace, similar expressions in the Virgin Islands. It was free at last; thank God I am free.

Later that night, I witnessed another event that was unlike anything I had seen before. Pat (not her real name) was a zealous sister, whom I was familiar with from other church events I had ministered at. She wanted to get involved with the prayer line, and I think she was hoping to be able to operate in the level of anointing for works of miracles and deliverance. I had often advised those who wished to participate in such a capacity to consider their spiritual state before getting involved. As we prayed for one of the ladies in attendance, who also was recognized as demonic, Pat came and placed her hand on her shoulder, and suddenly an apparent spiritual transfer took place. Pat was thrown to the floor and began twisting and hissing like a snake. I wish I had words to describe what I saw that night, but I don't. It was a startling sight; many attendees bolted for the door while others hugged the church walls in fear. But I was ready. I rebuked the spirit, and it left her almost immediately.

Pat looked shocked and terrified. It was a wake-up call for her, and I don't remember ever seeing her at any other deliverance service. I still get chills thinking about that evening.

This was a demonstration of spirit hopping, sometimes called spiritual transfer. These transfers happen all the time, unknown to many, especially during sexual encounters. One must always be mindful of their surroundings and relational encounters and especially their spiritual condition. Here is one more story before I move on, and I hope you will learn something about demonic behaviors from these testimonials. I was in Mourne Diablo (Mountain of Devils) Trinidad. We had a tent crusade, and one night a demon-possessed man walked in from the back and interrupted the service. He came down the center aisle and came straight to the front and stood in front of the preacher in an apparent challenge to him. The preacher was from New York, and I had only just met him on that trip. I didn't know much about his background, but he was obviously stunned. No one expected it. But why didn't we? I stood in the rear of the platform, watching it all play out. It quickly became clear that the minister was unfamiliar with the situation he was facing. So, I stepped forward and asked them to allow me to handle it. I stepped down from the platform onto the ground and stood face to face with the demon. For a moment, we both stared. It was like a duel from an old western film, where God faces the devil, evil versus good, the demonic, and I. It was going down, and the future of our tent meetings hung in the balance. I commanded the evil spirit to leave in the name of Jesus, and the man fell lifeless to the ground. Moments later, there was a scream from somewhere nearby. We did not know what was happening, but screams were coming from the home next to the tent. What we did not know soon became apparent, as a woman was brought in kicking and screaming. She did not want to be there, and I realized that this was a second encounter with the same Spirit I had just rebuked. It was obvious now that we were in a spiritual war zone. She was a middle- aged woman who was sitting at home when suddenly she was taken over by this Spirit. It was like a scene from the movie Fallen, starring Denzel Washington. Once again, I spoke to the demon, and it left, and the lady came to herself.

Phew! There was a nervous calm that followed. Who is next? You could almost hear the people's thoughts bouncing from the canopy of the yellow and white tent as we all held our breath. Was the Spirit gone for good? It seemed to have had enough for the night since there were no further manifestations that night, but I left knowing that the spirit still lived in the town.

Can Christians Have Demons?

Many have conjectured about whether or not demons can 'possess' or 'influence 'believers. While the Bible is silent concerning Christians being 'possessed,' it has much to say concerning demons' possible influence on us and of our need to be aware of their desire to affect our walk with God adversely.

The short answer is no. Satan, and his demons may tempt us, but they cannot dwell within us. Demons and the Holy Spirit will never dwell together in the same person. What business does darkness have with light? Here are some helpful scriptures.

According to the Scripture, the Holy Spirit indwells in every believer. John 14:15-17 "If you love me, you will keep my commandments. And I will ask the Father, and he will give you another Helper, to be with you forever, even the Spirit of truth, whom the world cannot receive, because it neither sees him nor knows him. You know him, for he dwells with you and will be in you."

Additionally, Jesus says in verse 23: *"If anyone loves me, he will keep my word, and my Father will love him, and we will come to him and make our home with him."*

Not only does the Holy Spirit dwell in every Christian, but the Father and the Son, through the Spirit, dwell in every Christian. No demon, nor the devil himself, can reside in a Christian if the Father and the Son and the Holy Spirit dwell in that Christian. Again! God and the devil cannot live in the same place or in the same person. God emphasizes in His Word that the Holy Spirit lives within those who have repented of their sins, have accepted Jesus as their savior, and have therefore been born into the family of God.

You, however, are not in the flesh but in the Spirit if, in fact, the Spirit of God dwells in you. Anyone who does not have the Spirit of Christ does not belong to him, (Romans 8:9). The Holy Spirit who lives in a born-again child of God bears witness with that person's spirit that he is a child of God. If the devil or a demon lived in that Christian and possessed that

Christian, the Holy Spirit could neither dwell in that person nor bear witness that such a person was a child of God.

CHAPTER 7

THE SOURCE OF DARK POWER

How art thou fallen from Heaven, O Lucifer, son of the morning! How art thou cut down to the ground, which didst weaken the nations! For thou hast said in thine heart, I will ascend into Heaven, I will exalt my throne above the stars of God: I will sit also upon the mount of the congregation, in the sides of the north: I will ascend above the heights of the clouds; I will be like the most High. Yet thou shalt be brought down to hell, to the sides of the pit.

Isaiah 14:12-15

Son of man, take up a lamentation upon the king of Tyrus, and say unto him, thus saith the Lord God; Thou sealest up the sum, full of wisdom, and perfect in beauty. Thou hast been in Eden the garden of God; every precious stone was thy covering, the sardius, topaz, and the diamond, the beryl, the onyx, and the jasper, the sapphire, the emerald, and the carbuncle, and gold: the workmanship of thy tabrets and of thy pipes was prepared in thee in the day that thou wast created. Thou art the anointed cherub that covereth; and I have set thee so: thou wast upon the holy mountain of God; thou hast walked up and down in the midst of the stones of fire. Thou wast perfect in thy ways from the day that thou wast created, till iniquity was found in thee. By the multitude of thy merchandise, they have filled the midst of thee with violence, and thou hast sinned: therefore, I will cast thee as profane out of the mountain of God: and I will destroy thee, O covering cherub, from the midst of the stones of fire. Thine heart was lifted up because of thy beauty, thou hast corrupted thy wisdom by reason of thy brightness: I will cast thee to the ground, I will lay thee before kings, that they may behold thee. Thou hast defiled thy sanctuaries by the multitude of thine iniquities, by the iniquity of thy traffick; therefore, will I bring forth a fire from the midst of thee, it shall devour thee, and I will bring thee to ashes upon the earth in the sight of all of them that behold thee. All they that know thee among the people shall be astonished at thee: thou shalt be a terror, and never shalt thou be any more.

Ezekiel 28:12-19, KJV

These two biblical passages also reference the king of Babylon, the King of Tyre, and the spiritual power behind the kings.

What caused Satan to be cast out from Heaven? He fell because of pride that originated from his desire to be God instead of a servant of God. Satan was the highest of all the angels, but he wasn't happy. He desired to be God and to rule the universe, and so God cast him out of Heaven as a fallen angel.

Who is Satan?

Satan is often caricatured as a red-horned, trident-raising cartoon villain; no wonder people may think of him like a movie character in the likes of Batman or the Green Goblin. His existence, however, is not based on fantasy. It is verified in the same book that narrates Jesus' life and death. You can find reference to him in the following scriptures:

1 Now, the serpent was more crafty than any of the wild animals the LORD God had made. He said to the woman, "Did God really say, 'You must not eat from any tree in the garden'?" 2 The woman said to the serpent, "We may eat fruit from the trees in the garden, 3 but God did say, 'You must not eat fruit from the tree that is in the middle of the garden, and you must not touch it, or you will die.'" 4 "You will not certainly die," the serpent said to the woman. 5 "For God knows that when you eat from it your eyes will be opened, and you will be like God, knowing good and evil." 6 When the woman saw that the fruit of the tree was good for food and pleasing to the eye, and also desirable for gaining wisdom, she took some and ate it. She also gave some to her husband, who was with her, and he ate it. 7 Then the eyes of both of them were opened, and they realized they were naked; so, they sewed fig leaves together and made coverings for themselves. 8 Then the man and his wife heard the sound of the LORD God as he was walking in the garden in the cool of the day, and they hid from the LORD God among the trees of the garden. 9 But the LORD God called to the man, "Where are you?" 10 He answered, "I heard you in the garden, and I was afraid because I was naked; so, I hid." 11 And he said, "who told you that you were naked? Have you eaten from the tree that I commanded you not to eat from?" 12 The man said, "The woman you put here with me—she gave me some fruit from the tree, and I ate it." 13 Then the LORD God said to the woman, "What is this you have done?" The woman said, "The serpent deceived me, and I ate." 14 So the LORD God said to the serpent, "Because you have done this, "Cursed are you above all livestock and all wild animals! You will crawl on your belly, and you will eat dust all the days of your life. 15 And I will put enmity between you and the woman, and between your offspring and hers; he will crush your head, and you will strike his heel." 16 To the woman he said, "I will make your pains in childbearing very severe; with painful labor you will give birth to children. Your desire will be for your husband, and he will rule over you."

Genesis 3:1-16:

12 "How you are fallen from Heaven, O Lucifer, son of the morning! How you are cut down to the ground, you who weakened the nations! 13 For you have said in your heart: 'I will ascend into Heaven, I will exalt my throne above the stars of God; I will also sit on the mount of the congregation on the farthest sides of the north; 14 I will ascend above the heights of the clouds, I will be like the Most High.' 15 Yet you shall be brought down to Sheol, to the lowest depths of the Pit.

Isaiah 14:12-15:

12 "Son of man, take up a lamentation for the king of Tyre, and say to him, 'Thus says the Lord God: "You were the seal of perfection, Full of wisdom and perfect in beauty. 13 You were in Eden, the garden of God; Every precious stone was your covering: The sardius, topaz, and diamond, Beryl, onyx, and jasper, Sapphire, turquoise, and emerald with gold. The workmanship of your timbrels and pipes Was prepared for you on the day you were created. 14 "You were the anointed cherub who covers. I established you; You were on the holy mountain of God; You walked back and forth in the midst of fiery stones. 15 You were perfect in your ways from the day you were created, till iniquity was found in you. 16 "By the abundance of your trading. You became filled with violence within, and you sinned; Therefore, I cast you as a profane thing Out of the mountain of God; And I destroyed you, O covering cherub, From the midst of the fiery stones. 17 "Your heart was (a)lifted up because of your beauty; You corrupted your wisdom for the sake of your splendor; I cast you to the ground, I laid you before kings, that they might gaze at you. 18 "You defiled your sanctuaries. By the multitude of your iniquities, By the iniquity of your trading; Therefore I brought fire from your midst; It devoured you, And I turned you to ashes upon the earth In the sight of all who saw you. 19 All who knew you among the peoples are astonished at you; You have become a horror, And shall be no more forever."

Ezekiel 28:12-19:

Then Jesus, being filled with the Holy Spirit, returned from the Jordan, and was led by the Spirit into the wilderness, being tempted for forty days by the devil. And in those days, He ate nothing, and afterward, when they had ended, He was hungry. And the devil said to Him, "If You are the Son of God, command this stone to become bread." But Jesus answered him, saying, "It is written, 'Man shall not live by bread alone, but by every word of God.'" Then the devil, taking Him up on a high mountain, showed Him all the kingdoms of the world in a moment of time. And the devil said to Him. "All this authority I will give you, and their glory; for this has been delivered to me, and I give it to whomever I wish. Therefore, if you will worship before me, all will be yours." And Jesus answered and said to him, "Get behind Me, Satan! For it is written, "You shall worship the Lord your God, and Him only you shall serve." Then he brought Him to Jerusalem, set Him on the pinnacle of the temple, and said to Him, "If you are the Son of God, throw yourself down from here. For it is written: 'He shall give His angels charge over you, to keep you,' and, 'In their hands they shall bear you up, lest you dash your foot against a stone.'" And Jesus answered and said to him, "It has been said, 'You shall not tempt the Lord your God.'"

Matthew 4:1-11:

Satan is the leader of all the fallen angels. These demons, which exist in the invisible spiritual realm, still affect our physical world through rebellion, sickness, and evil action through demonic possession. Satan masquerades as an "angel of light," deceiving humans just as he deceived Eve in the beginning.

(Genesis 3).

Jesus himself testified of Satan's existence. During his ministry, he personally faced temptation from the devil (Matthew 4:1-11), cast out demons possessing people (Luke 8:27-33), and defeated the evil one and his Legion of demon angels at the cross. Christ also helped us understand the ongoing, spiritual war between God and Satan, good and evil.

(Isaiah 14:12-15; Luke 10:17-20).

With Jesus Christ on our side, we need not fear Satan's limited power (Hebrew 2:14-15). We should be wise, however, in resisting his tactics:

"For though we live in the world, we do not wage war as the world does. The weapons we fight with are not the weapons of the world. On the contrary, they have divine power to demolish strongholds. We demolish arguments and every pretension that sets itself up against the knowledge of God, and we take captive every thought to make it obedient to Christ."

(2 Corinthians 10:3-5).

Throughout the history of Satan, evil has been his identity because he is directly opposite of God's character. God's holy standard found in the Bible exposes evil. If we do not rely on its truth, we can easily err in the following ways:

- Denying satan's existence
- Fearfully focusing on satan rather than on Christ Jesus who overcame him.
- *Worshipping satan, preferring the darkness of evil rather than the light that reveals sin* (John 3:19; 2 Corinthians 11:14-15). *And no wonder! For satan himself transforms himself into an angel of light.*

15 Therefore it is no great thing if his ministers also transform themselves into ministers of righteousness, whose end will be according to their works.

Any of these approaches please the devil. He wants us to deny, fear, obey, or worshiping him. Unless we follow the trustworthy source, the Bible, he will deceive us.

> "Finally, my brethren, be strong in the Lord and in the power of His might. Put on the whole armor of God, that you may be able to stand against the wiles of the devil."
>
> (Ephesians 6:10-11)

In our scientific, rational age, spiritual beliefs are scorned as myths. Satan, however, doesn't mind those who rebuff the reality of fallen angels or demons. By masking himself, he can tempt and deceive people without blame. The wise will never forget that satan and demons, determined to deceive humans, are fighting real battles and wars against heavenly angels.

Satan compels or entices his prey to follow him whether they realize it or not. Maybe they are simply ignorant and confused. Many would rather believe in human theory than obey divine revelation and natural law. Whether blind, bound, or brazenly willing, they join Satan for a doomed destiny. They condemn themselves to eternity in hell.

While Satan is more powerful than we humans, God doesn't leave us defenseless. We are assured of this in Ephesians 6:10-11; at the Lord's rebuke, satan and his demons shudder and flee *James 2:19; You believe that there is one God. You do well. Even the demons believe - and tremble!* When Jesus Christ died, He overcame them (Jude1:9). Colossians 2:15 Having disarmed principalities and powers, He made a public spectacle of them, triumphing over them in it. Only in the authority of Jesus does anyone have the power to stand against the devil. Those saved from sin by Jesus' death on the cross are protected; those who are not saved from Satan's power perish with him (John 3:16; 1 Peter 5:8-10).

Referencing Satan

There is a belief going around in some circles in the church that suggests we should not talk about Satan or the "enemy." Jesus never teaches this doctrine. In fact, Jesus mentions satan and the enemy several times in the gospels. Obviously, we do not focus on the enemy; we focus on Christ. However, any warrior or army will tell you that knowing the enemy is essential for warfare. If an army does not know its enemy, that army is in great danger of losing the battle and being crushed.

Does Satan Have the Power to Create?

There have been a number of leaders who say that satan does not have creative power. These same leaders say that sickness and disease are not from God because He can't give what He does not have. If sickness and disease are not from God, then they must be from satan. But how can they be from satan if satan does not have the power to create? So, are sickness and disease from God or Satan? Does satan have the power to create or not? Clearly, the doctrine being taught in the church does not add up. I will leave the reader to meditate on this line of thought.

Deception

One of satan's primary weapons against us is deception. Deception is a power. Someone can only be deceived by Satan even if he or she is a believer in Christ. Once a believer is deceived into any area of compromise, authority can be exercised over the believer by satan. This is exactly what happened to Eve. It serves to remind all believers that God's word is truth and any deviation from it is dangerous and potentially deadly.

CHAPTER 8

SPIRITUAL WARFARE

Ephesians 6: 10- 11 says, "Finally, my brethren, be strong in the Lord and in the power of His might. 11 Put on the whole armor of God, that you may be able to stand against the wiles of the devil." The devil is a trickster - a very good one, and the Bible says you have to wear the armor of God so that you may be able to survive his tricks. You cannot do the same things that others do and expect a different result. There are a number of people today who are living through hell after they've retired. You can't do the same old thing and fall into the same old trick that devil's been using forever and expect a different outcome, that is not smart thinking. The Bible says we must be able to stand against the trickery of the devil. Ephesians 6:12 says, "For we do not wrestle against flesh and blood, but against principalities, against powers, against the rulers of the darkness of this age, against spiritual hosts of wickedness in the heavenly places."

We're not fighting flesh and blood; the problem is that we spend most of our time fighting with the wrong enemy. We fight with our spouses, our children, our bosses, with our pastors; everywhere we go, we are fighting. We are fighting the wrong battle and the wrong opponent because behind those behaviors, behind those irritations, is the working of demonic forces speaking to people's minds and having them give you hell. And so, while we're fighting each other, the enemy is sitting in the corner having a laugh party because that's exactly what he wants. We curse each other and fight with each other, and yet coming together in agreement against our common enemy is the very source of our strength and authority. The Bible says in (Matt 18:19),

> *"Again, I say to you that if two of you agree on earth concerning anything that they ask, it will be done for them by My Father in heaven."*

But then we spend so much time fighting with the little demons that are triggering the challenges we're dealing with every day, forgetting that we are not fighting against flesh and blood - flesh and blood is not our problem! So, what are we fighting against?

The Bible lays it out for us; it says we are fighting against principalities, against powers, and against the rulers of the darkness of this world and against spiritual wickedness in high places (Eph. 6:12). That's what we're fighting against, not flesh and blood. Sometimes you're fighting, and you do not even know why you're fighting, and that is the work of demons. How do people go from playing domino to chopping off each other's heads? Remember, we wrestle not against flesh and blood but against principalities and powers and spiritual wickedness. If that is the case, then we need to have a strategy. The famous boxer George Foreman - one of the greatest of all times - knocked every opponent out within 3-4 rounds; you never went past six rounds with George Foreman in the ring. Then he had a fight with a guy named Mohammed Ali. Ali had studied Foreman's fighting technique, and what he did in the gym was practice how to take punches, and hang in there, because he was working on a strategy. And so, when Foreman and Ali had their fight, Foreman started to throw his usual punches, and Mohammed Ali just kept taking them, he wasn't fighting, and people began to wonder what was wrong with him - he wasn't fighting back, he put up with it, and he allowed Foreman to get in as many blows as possible, and he blocked and ran around in the ring, until after about the 7th round; then be began to *move like a butterfly and sting like a bee* and knocked Foreman out.

At the end of the fight, someone said, 'Mohammed, explain to us what was going on out there.' Mohammed said, 'well, I studied George Foreman, and I realized that he had never fought anybody past six rounds and so I figured that if I could take some blows and save my energy past the sixth round, then I'd get my chance to knock the daylight out of him because after six rounds he doesn't have much left in him and then it's time for me to sting like a bee. Strategy! - you've got to have a strategy. The reason why the devil is beating you up is because you don't have a strategy, and so this book is to give you a strategy of how to win the battle against the enemy. So, who are our enemies? We will examine them in the following chapters.

CHAPTER 9

ENEMY NUMBER 1 - PRINCIPALITIES

A principality is a ranked demon. A principality is defined as a state ruled by a prince, usually a relatively small state or a state that falls within a larger state, such as an empire. As such, a principality is actually not a fallen angel itself but the seat of authority or the region that the fallen angel has authority over. A prince rules over a principality. Daniel: 10 makes it very clear that fallen angels and angels from God are both called princes:

> *But the prince of the kingdom of Persia withstood me twenty-one days, and behold, Michael, one of the chief princes, came to help me, for I had been left alone there with the kings of Persia,*
>
> (Daniel 10:13 NKJV).

In this Scripture, an angel of the Lord visits Daniel. This is not the angel Gabriel that visited Daniel in chapters 8 and 9. The angel tells Daniel that the prince (fallen angel) over Persia withstood him for 21 days. Then the angel states that Prince Michael came to help him. It is worthy to note that the devil had studied God's operation. He learned a lot of things while he was in Heaven, and so when he was cast out, he established order in his own ranking, he established principalities. They are ranked officers that are in charge of a number of other operations and work together. Think of the US military – you have the Army, the Navy, the Air force, etc. Take the Navy for instance, there are different operations in the Navy, but they are all related to water – they all have water in common, if you're in the Air force, it's all air related but you have different operations in the Air force and so they are ranked together; so it is with principalities. When Satan rebelled against the throne, he seduced one-third of the angels to come with him. These angels do not have the same place in Heaven. However, they do maintain their seats of authority in a heavenly place over the earth. The following Scripture in Revelation shows us that a third of the angels had fallen *"...And war broke out in Heaven: Michael and his angels fought with the dragon, and the dragon and his angels fought, but they did not prevail, nor was a place found for them in Heaven any longer. So, the great dragon was cast out, that serpent of old called the Devil and Satan, who deceives the whole world; he was cast to the earth, and his angels were cast out with him" (Revelation 12:7-9 NKJV).*

However, the angels that had fallen are not confined on the earth as some may want to believe, but their power is confined in the regions outside of Heaven.

There are three head demons:

1. Demon over Moral Impurity

This demon entails everything that deals with uncleanness, everything that deals with fornication, adultery, and homosexuality. All these kinds of behavior fall under… moral impurity. They have demons that are ranked and work together. When you work with people, you understand that you never see someone who has an issue in one area that doesn't have an issue in another. Bring me somebody who loves and watches pornography and tell me that you won't find somebody who is trying to act out that behavior or some of those behaviors in some other way. These demons are designed to pull you down.

2. Demon of Bitterness

There are a lot of people who do not understand how deadly bitterness is. The Bible tells us in Heb.12:15, "looking carefully lest anyone fall short of the grace of God; lest any root of bitterness springing up cause trouble, and by this many become defiled."

There are some people who cannot separate themselves from an event, and they get bitter and angry, and bitterness and envy open the door to so many other things to come in and torment your life. And so, you can't have a successful relationship, you have anger issues, you can't keep a job, and all kinds of things are happening in your life because you're just a bitter person, as a result no one wants to be around you. This has a devastating result as every person's destiny is somehow tied to another person's existence.

3. Demon of Temporal Values

This is the demon that causes people to value the things of the world more than the things of God. Half of the problem a lot of people have in the world is because they do not value the things of God. Their worth is based on how much money they have, how many houses and cars they have, what position they hold at work, how many degrees they have. They are lost and confused because they are focusing on temporal things, which are not designed to last and are not relevant when it comes to your eternity. But somehow, the enemy deceives you every day to focus on the things that are temporal – "I have to fix that car today"; "I have to clean the house before I go to church," and so on. You do everything except that which is related to God; we put everything in line before God. There is a demon at work in your life, causing you to see things through those lenses – temporal values lies. The problem is we spend our time fighting with the little demons instead of dealing with the 'big boys because once we take care of the big boys, all the little ones will be gone with them. If we deal with moral impurity, we don't have to worry about adultery, fornication and pornography. All these demons are ranked according to purpose.

Power of united prayer against principalities

Lev.26:7 says, "You will chase your enemies, and they shall fall by the sword before you." In order words, he says two of us can put ten thousand to flight. The problem, however, is that we do not want to get together when it comes to prayer. You are too lazy to get up and come to prayer, but I bet if you had to do overtime, you would get up and go. That is the demon; he is playing games with your mind, telling you, 'Oh, you're too tired.' 'You need rest.' The Lord said if we can agree touching anything, then we can put a thousand to flight. What is God saying to us? I believe God wants us to know that it is important that we have accountability. The problem is that the devil has convinced us that we cannot share our struggles because it is our personal business, and no one can be trusted to know. Why does the enemy want you to keep your struggle to yourself? The answer is because he knows there is power in agreement and sin's struggle persists when it is kept in the dark. That is why we all need accountability partners, someone you can call and say, 'stand with me. I'm about to fall; I'm struggling. Please help.'

4. Principalities still hold authority

We should note that Paul says in Ephesians 6:12 that we struggle against principalities in heavenly places. My first point is that we are currently in conflict with them. My second point is that this scripture was written after Jesus rose from the dead. My third point is that these principalities are still in heavenly places and have not yet been trapped on the earth. The word for principality in Greek also means magistrate, power, and rule. The word for powers in Greek also means authority, jurisdiction, power, rights, and strength. Principalities and powers clearly still hold power and authority, as their names suggest. There are many people in the body of Christ who have misunderstood the scriptures. These people believe that Jesus removed satan's power and authority at the cross and that principalities have been dis-empowered. This is simply not true, and this false doctrine can be harmful to the body of Christ. We will examine the facts as presented in the scriptures to determine the truth:

> *For He has not put the world to come, of which we speak, in subjection to angels. But one testified in a certain place, saying: "What is man that You are mindful of him, Or the son of man that You take care of him? You have made him a little lower than the angels; You have crowned him with glory and honor and set him over the works of Your hands. You have put all things in subjection under his feet." For in that He put all in subjection under him, He left nothing that is not put under him. But now, we do not yet see all things put under him.*
>
> *Hebrews 2:5-8 (NKJV)*

The Scripture states that man was made a little lower than the angels, and all things were put in subjection to him, but man currently does not see all things (including the fallen angels) put under his feet and is currently wrestling against principalities and powers as Paul states.

> *But even if our gospel is veiled, it is veiled to those who are perishing, whose minds the God of this age has blinded, who do not believe, lest the light of the gospel of the glory of Christ, who is the image of God, should shine on them.*
>
> *2 Corinthians 4:3-4 (NKJV)*

This Scripture was clearly written after Jesus died on the cross. The Holy Spirit, speaking through Paul, calls satan the god of this age. Meaning, satan will maintain his status as the "god of this age" until Jesus Christ personally removes him at the very end of this age.

1 Corinthians 15: 23-25 (NKJV) But each one in his own order: Christ the first fruits, afterward those who are Christ's at His coming. Then comes the end, when He delivers the kingdom to God the Father, when He puts an end to all rule and all authority and power. For He must reign till He has put all enemies under His feet.

The above Scripture indicates that Jesus will not put an end to evil powers and authorities (principalities and powers) until His return to the earth.

Now the beast which I saw was like a leopard, his feet were like the feet of a bear, and his mouth like the mouth of a lion. The dragon gave him his power, his throne, and great authority. And he was given a mouth speaking great things and blasphemies, and he was given authority to continue for forty-two months. It was granted to him to make war with the saints and to overcome them. And authority was given him over every tribe, tongue, and nation.

Revelation 13:2, 5, 7 (NKJV)

This scripture shows that satan still has "great authority" until the end of this age. satan will give the antichrist his throne and power. The antichrist will have this authority over the whole world for three and a half years. He will make war against believers and overcome them by killing them during this period. It is very clear from the scriptures that the Lord has not yet taken satan's power and authority away. Addressing satan and his principalities must be handled with care. Satan was created by God; he is very skilled at taking out leaders. He used a woman to bring down the spiritual giant King David. A tactic satan has used time and time again throughout the centuries. To be disrespectful to fallen angelic majesty is completely stupid. Observe the following texts:

Likewise, also these dreamers defile the flesh, reject authority, and speak evil of dignitaries. Yet Michael the archangel, in contending with the devil, when he disputed about the body of Moses, dared not bring against him a reviling accusation, but said, "The Lord rebuke you!" (Jude 1:8-9 NKJV)...and especially those who walk according to the flesh in the lust of uncleanness and despise authority. They are presumptuous, self- willed. They are not afraid to speak evil of dignitaries, whereas angels, who are greater in power and might, do not bring a reviling accusation against them before the Lord. – (2 Peter 2:10-11 NKJV)

Michael, who is greater in power and might than satan, did not speak evil of him. He simply told satan, "The Lord rebuke you!" We can learn from these examples how to handle satan. Remember that man has no power of himself that can stand the brute force of the devil. Neither can he protect himself from the onslaught of satan; he must be completely dependent on God.

Elijah and Jezebel

To understand the seriousness of principalities, we will look at the life of Elijah. Elijah challenged the fallen prince over Israel by making a mockery of Baal and slaying the prophets of Baal (1 Kings 18). Here is the account after these events: *And Ahab told Jezebel all that Elijah had done, also how he had executed all the prophets with the sword. Then Jezebel sent a messenger to*

Elijah, saying, "So let the gods do to me, and more also, if I do not make your life as the life of one of them by tomorrow about this time." And when he saw that, he arose and ran for his life, and went to Beersheba, which belongs to Judah, and left his servant there, (I Kings19:1-3 NKJV).

Elijah took his eyes off the Lord and put his eyes on the evil prince with a nationwide principality. The pressure of this fallen angel must have been extremely severe to cause confusion and fear in this seasoned prophet. I will not justify the actions of Elijah. However, if we were in the same situation, what would we have done? Very few people have stood toe to toe with a national principality. Most Christians can't even stand against a little demon. Can you imagine the entire power and force of the United States government coming after you? That's exactly what Elijah faced. Even though Elijah had already been protected and hidden once by the Lord (1 Kings 17), he forgot that the One who protects him is much greater than the fallen angel that was coming after him. He forgot that the Lord breaks the mountains by His mighty power, causes earthquakes, and sends fire upon the earth. No one or no principality can stand before the Lord God Almighty.

Thorn in the Flesh

And lest I should be exalted above measure by the abundance of the revelations, a thorn in the flesh was given to me, a messenger of Satan to buffet me, lest I be exalted above measure, (2 Corinthians 12:7 NKJV). There has been much debate in the church about Paul's "thorn in the flesh." We must look at the meaning of the Greek word "messenger" and the context of the Scripture to determine what the thorn was. The Greek word used for messenger is "aggelos." This word means angel. This Greek word is translated as "angel" 178 times in the New Testament. It is only translated as "messenger" seven times. This word should be translated "angel" in 2 Corinthians 12:7.

A fallen angel of Satan was sent by Satan to buffet Paul. The Lord allowed this to keep Paul humble. The context of the scripture defines the "buffeting" or afflictions this fallen angel was causing in Paul's life:

Therefore, I take pleasure in weaknesses, in injuries, in necessities, in persecutions, in distresses, for Christ's sake. For when I am weak, then am I strong, (2 Corinthians 12:10). The thorn in the flesh was not a physical disease. The angel of Satan stirred up persecution and turmoil everywhere Paul went. Paul was thrown out of cities, beaten, stoned, and went through much physical suffering on account of this fallen angel.

Hindrance by Principalities.

Principalities over cities, regions, and nations are hindering revival. These fallen angels promote dullness, darkness, and spiritual lethargy. The reason the church is not experiencing "open Heavens" is because of these angels. Principalities will not face their final judgment until after Jesus returns to the earth. However, they can be temporarily judged at times in this age. A fallen angel over a region or country may be bound for a time if the courts of Heaven have so determined. The great revival in Argentina occurred because the principality was bound over the nation. People were suddenly open to the gospel, pastors and evangelists were moving in remarkable miracles, people were rushing to meetings, crusades, and churches to be healed and to be saved. The nation went from being hardened to God to being open to the gospel. It was like a light switch. Once the fallen angel was bound, the Heavens opened over Argentina, and a light shone all over the nation. Binding principality is a major key to revival.

Engaging Principalities

We should never engage principalities in spiritual warfare on our own. The exception to this would be if the Lord commanded you to engage the principality. To try and bind a fallen angel in our own strength and our own timing is acting independently of the Lord. Engaging in battle against a principality without a direct word from the Lord can be dangerous. If someone is acting independently of the Lord, He may not protect that person. This can lead to the person getting into an accident, developing a sickness, falling into sin, or losing their life. If you engage a principality and the enemy has something on you, that principality will sift you like wheat. If you engage a fallen angel without God's permission and protection, the enemy will have legal right to strike you. It is important to be completely at an elevated state in your relationship with Jesus Christ before engaging in spiritual warfare. Warfare is not for novices. When Christ is truly operating in His overcomers, the following scripture will become a reality and not just a doctrine.

Seated with Christ …which He worked in Christ when He raised Him from the dead and seated Him at His right hand in the heavenly places, far above all principality and power and might and dominion, and every name that is named, not only in this age but also in that which is to come, (Ephesians 1:20-21 NKJV) and raised us up together, and made us sit together in the heavenly places in Christ Jesus, (Ephesians 2:6 NKJV). Christ, as a man, was ranked far above principalities and powers. We are raised up to sit in Heaven with Christ (the word "places" is added by the translator). Therefore, believers (whom the Lord has made this revelation real in their hearts) outrank fallen angels because Christ lives in a believer. This is why we are struggling against principalities and powers. They still have authority, and we have authority. The fallen angels are fighting to keep their thrones and dominions, and we are imperfect vessels trying to learn how to operate in our authority. We must also understand that Christ has left these principalities empowered for a reason - for our training and maturing.

We must only use our authority under the direct guidance of the Holy Spirit. Jesus could have taken all power and authority from satan and his angels, but in His wisdom, He has allowed satan to retain it until the end of the age. Everyone on this earth will be able to choose who they will serve and who they will love. Because satan has kept his authority, the overcoming remnant bride will be made ready. The evil pressures and turmoil of this age will produce a remnant bride who is mature and capable of ruling with Christ in the millennium.

CHAPTER 10

ENEMY NUMBER 2 - POWERS

This has to do with ability, capacity, control, authority, and delegated influence. Here is the mistake that most people make. People are enthrall by power and often believe that all demonstration of power by someone is a manifestation of God's work. I have learned not to be excited about power but always seek understanding about what is behind the person's power. There are some people who will spend all night in a church service in anticipation to see demonstrations of power. These are folks who would never sit and listen to preaching for five hours. Often times I had witness people praising a so-call anointed man who has questionable character. Can I tell you that the devil has power? Many Christians today move about from church to church, looking for signs and miracles. What they fail to understand is that the devil has powers. It's not everything that you see powerful comes from Jehovah God.

I was an evangelist before becoming a pastor, and during those years, I'd seen God do many miracles, and the truth is that as I stood there ministering and watching these miracles, I was in awe like everybody else. I did not perform those miracles; they were the work of God. In other instances I had prayed until strength left my body and nothing happened. I came to realize then that God does miracles when he wants to. Be careful of your intrigue with miracles. You need to understand that the enemy has powers, and as such, a person can be easily misled by the devil. It is that same desire that often leads people to seek witch doctors because they operate with demonic powers. Powers are assigned influences that come to influence things around you. If the night were to turn into day, church going, so-called "Christians" would be ashamed of themselves because many, like Saul, will not wait for an answer from God. We can see this in 1 Samuel 13:8-14:

This must never be found among you. Remember, not everything that looks powerful comes from God. I'm excited to report to you that no such powers are a match to our God, so no weapon that is formed against you shall prosper; I'm excited to say to you that greater is He that is in you than he that is in the world, I'm excited to tell you that nobody can bewitch you if you are a child of God. You have the covering of God. There is no demon in hell that can touch you if you are a child of God. I'm here to tell you that my God is bigger; my God is stronger than any principality than any power. Since He is bigger and able to keep you from the wiles of the devil. Why not surrender your life to his care?

He waited seven days, the time set by Samuel; but Samuel did not come to Gilgal, and Saul's men began to scatter. 9 So he said, "Bring me the burnt offering and the fellowship offerings." And Saul offered up the burnt offering. 10 Just as he finished making the offering, Samuel arrived, and Saul went out to greet him.11 "What have you done?" asked Samuel. Saul replied, "When I saw that the men were scattering, and that you did not come at the set time, and that the Philistines were assembling at Mikmash, 12 I thought, 'Now the Philistines will come down against me at Gilgal, and I have not sought the Lord's favor.' So, I felt compelled to offer the burnt offering."13 "You have done a foolish thing," Samuel said. "You have not kept the command the Lord your God gave you; if you had, he would have established your kingdom over Israel for all time. 14 But now your kingdom will not endure; the Lord has sought out a man after his own heart and appointed him ruler of his people, because you have not kept the Lord's command."

CHAPTER 11

ENEMY NUMBER 3- RULERS OF DARKNESS

Continuing in his description of satan's rank and file in descending order, Paul mentions "the rulers of the darkness of this world." This amazing phrase is taken from the word kosmokrateros and is a compound of the words kosmos and kratos. The word kosmos denotes order or arrangement, whereas the word kratos has to do with raw power. Thus, the compounded word kosmokrateros depicts raw power that has been harnessed and put into some kind of order. This word kosmokrateros was at times used to depict military training camps where young men were assembled, trained, and turned into a mighty army. These young men were like raw power when they first arrived in the training camp. However, as the military training progressed and the new recruits were taught discipline and order, all that raw manpower was converted into an organized, disciplined army. This is the word Paul now uses in his description of satan's kingdom, and what does it mean?

It tells us that satan is so serious about doing damage to humanity that he deals with demon spirits as though they are troops! He puts them in ranks and files, gives those orders and assignments, and then sends them out like military soldiers who are committed to killing. Just as men in a human army are equipped and trained in their methods of destruction, so, too, are these demon spirits. Once these demons are trained and ready to start their assault, satan sends them forth to do their devious work against human beings.

Paul refers to this dispatch of evil spirits when he writes about "spiritual wickedness in high places." The word "Wickedness" is taken from the word poneros, and it is used to depict something that is bad, vile, malevolent, vicious, impious, and malignant. This tells us the ultimate aim of Satan's dark domain: These evil spirits are sent forth to afflict humanity in bad, vile, malevolent, and vicious ways! Satan uses all these evil forces in his attacks against mankind. Nevertheless, we believers have far more authority and power than the devil and his forces. You and I have the Greater One living within us! As members of the Church of Jesus Christ, we are loaded with heaps of raw power. The church has no shortage of power, nor is it deficient in God-given authority, and we have more power and authority than all the evil forces combined. What we lack, however, is order and discipline. We must learn to see ourselves as the army of God and to view the local church as the training center where we are taught to do God's business. Then we must heed the call of Jesus and be dispatched into the dark world to preach the gospel and to drive these evil forces from people's lives. We must buckle down and begin to view ourselves as the troops of Jesus Christ!

Being organized and disciplined includes living a holy and consecrated life. There is no room for laziness in the life of a real Christian soldier. To deal with these forces that are being dispatched to destroy us and the world around us, it is required that we walk with God and listen to the voice of His Spirit. We must gird up the loins of our minds and fill our thoughts with the Word of God. Satan's troops are serious — and if we are not serious about our contest with them, it will only be a matter of time until they discover our weakness and strike with all their forces to bring us down. Be determined to see yourself as a soldier in the army of God. Do not allow anything to remain in your life that would hinder your fight of faith. Be disciplined, committed, and organized. Take advantage of all the weapons described in Ephesians 6:13-18, and then get ready to witness the awesome demonstration of God's power in your life as you prevail against satan's rank and file.

CHAPTER 12

ENEMY NUMBER 4 - SPIRITUAL WICKEDNESS IN HIGH PLACES

The 'spiritual powers' are not spiritual principles, but 'spiritual hosts' of wickedness; corresponding to 'the power of the air in Ephesians 2:2, "…… the ways of this world and of the ruler of the kingdom of the air, the spirit who is now at work in those who are disobedient," and the phrase 'in the heavenly places,' stands obviously in antithesis to 'the darkness of this world.' In this sense, and in all other cases seems to be logical.

Ephesians 1:3: "Blessed be the God and Father of our Lord Jesus Christ, who has blessed us with every spiritual blessing in heavenly places in Christ." The spiritual hosts of evil are described as fighting in the region above the earth. But the meaning underlying this figure surely points to the power of evil as directly spiritual, not acting through physical and human agency, but attacking the spirit in that higher aspect, in which it contemplates heavenly things and ascends to communion with God. As the former idea corresponds to the gross work of temptation on the high mountain, so this to the subtler spiritual temptation on the pinnacle of the temple. It is the enemy's desire that you take your focus off Jehovah and give attention and glory to him, satan.

Principalities and demons always work together; they almost always appear in scriptures together. Rom 8:38 says, "For I am persuaded that neither death nor life, nor angels nor principalities nor powers, nor things present nor things to come, nor height nor depth, nor any other created thing, shall be able to separate us from the love of God which is in Christ Jesus our Lord."

I'm excited about this verse because there is nothing that the enemy can do or say about me that will divorce me from the never ending love of God. Let me say it another way, "There is nothing that you can do in your life that will stop God from loving you." It doesn't matter how low you get or what you've done and it doesn't matter what people say about you. The Bible says that no demon in hell is going to be able to stop God from loving you. John 15: 13 says, "Greater love has no one than this than to lay down one's life for his friends." It is not that we love God but that he first loved us. It doesn't matter how dirty you are, no sin that you have committed, the greater the sin, the greater the grace of God. Are excited about the love of God that brought you out of your mess, lifted you up, and turned your life around? I can brag about God because He loves me. All of us are guilty of moral failures but thank God we are justified by the work of Jesus Christ on the cross, the price of our sins are fully paid and he has wiped away all transgressions!'

Eph. 1:15-20 : "Therefore I also, after I heard of your faith in the Lord Jesus and your love for all the saints, do not cease to give thanks for you, making mention of you in my prayers: that the God of our Lord Jesus Christ, the Father of glory, may give to you the Spirit of wisdom and revelation in the knowledge of Him, the eyes of your understanding being enlightened; that you may know what is the hope of His calling, what are the riches of the glory of His inheritance in the saints, and what is the exceeding greatness of His power toward us who believe, according to the working of His mighty power which He worked in Christ when He raised Him from the dead and seated Him at His right hand in the heavenly places, far above all principality and power and might and dominion, and every name that is named, not only in this age but also in that which is to come. And He put all things under His feet and gave Him to be head over all things to the church, which is His body, the fullness of Him who fills all in all."

The Bible says that when God saved us, He raised us up and established our authority in Christ. Let me explain to you what that means to us spiritually. The Scripture says that God gave him authority over principalities, that's over everything that you are fighting against your life, over the devil's high-ranking demons, even the low ranking, and middle-ranking demons. He set up Jesus far above principalities and gave Him a name that is above all names given to men in this world but also in the world that is to come. In other words, yesterday He was, today He is, and tomorrow His name will still carry unchallenged authority. He doesn't change. Jesus is still the one that the enemy must contend with and can never overcome.

God said, I'm going to raise him up, and I am going to put all things – your pain, your sorrows, everything you've been going through, your finances, the trouble in your marriage, your wayward children, your struggling business - I'm going to put all that under his feet. He made Christ to be the head, and he put the enemy - principalities, and powers under his feet and made him to be the head over all things, the church which is His body. What the Bible is saying is that Jesus is the head, and we are the body, and everything that the devil is throwing at us is under our feet because if it is under Jesus's feet, I am more than a conqueror in Him.

I don't know about you, but I have been fighting and wrestling with demons. And they come in packs, launching their assaults. When they show up in the church, they show up with trouble. The congregation becomes lethargic and impossible to mobilize; everybody is against everybody; conflicts and disunity arise over nonsensical issues. Have you ever been at a point in your life where you know the enemy is fighting against you, he messes with your finances, strikes your family, and depletes your business? Aren't you tired? You spend all that time wrestling with little demons, fighting with the people around you. Instead, you should be calling on the name of Jesus and declaring the word of God over your situation. Stand in the authority given to you through your relationship with Jesus Christ.

CHAPTER 13

THE ARMOR OF GOD

The word of God tells us that we must take up the whole armor of God; I cannot emphasize enough how important it is that you put on the whole armor of God every day. As I mentioned before, we are up against very powerful forces that are constantly at work to destroy the plan of God for our lives. You must dress yourself for battle at all times. As long as you are alive, there is going to attacks from the enemy constantly, and if the devil is allowed to have his way, he will destroy you. For that reason, we should dressed to withstand his assaults. In this section of the book, I will outline what the Bible outline to us as our defense and offense tools. I will address each part to make it relevant in our day and time.

What is the armor?

The armor is an extremely important part of a soldier's gear. Over the years, the design of armor has changed but the main goal has not, which is to protect whoever is wearing it during battle. In our world today, armors are made to protect from bullets, but in the past, particularly at the time of the writing of scripture, the Roman armor was designed to protect against swords, spears, arrows, and other projectiles. I will examine the significance and how it relates to us in today's world.

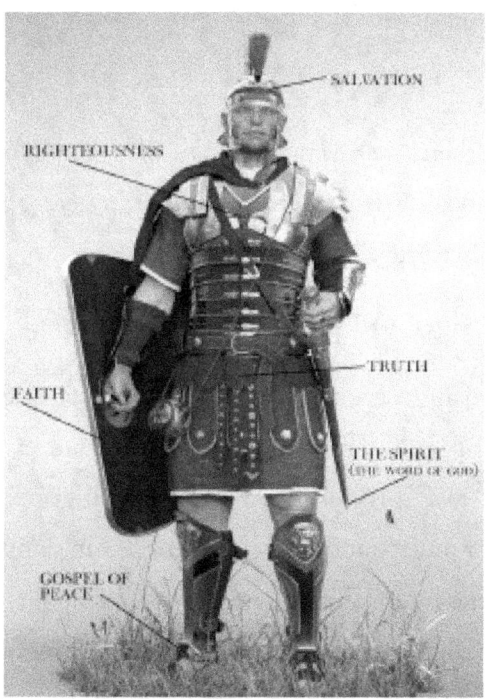

Roman Soldier in full armor

https://www.halliewrites.com/home/be-strong-in-the-lord

CHAPTER 14

THE BELT OF TRUTH

I believe there are seven principles of truth found in God's word; and I will briefly cover them here and presents supporting scripture verses.

1. Design and purpose

God created and designed everyone for a reason and a purpose. In fact, our purpose in life is the essence of our existence; and many times, we carry on ignorantly and suffer because we do not know or understand our own purpose and significance. We allow the enemy to fill our minds with lies about who we are or aren't, what we can or can't do. 1 Peter 2:9 reminds us that, "But you are a chosen people, a royal priesthood, a holy nation, God's special possession, that you may declare the praises of him who called you out of darkness into his wonderful light."

We are all chosen, and designed on purpose with a purpose by God, and He knows us through and through, as Jeremiah 29:11 says, For I know the plans I have for you," declares the LORD, "plans to prosper you and not to harm you, plans to give you hope and a future.

We should not live with the notation that our lives have no meaning or purpose. Remember that our God's plan for us is good and He works all things according to His purpose and plan. Nothing can happen without His knowledge or approval. Psalm 57:2 says, *"I cry out to God Most High, to God who fulfills his purpose for me."*

God has uniquely created you, and has great plans for you, and will fulfill every purpose He has for you. Do not allow the enemy to deceive you and take your joy away. Psalm 139:14, says, *"I will praise thee; for I am fearfully and wonderfully made: marvelous are thy works; and that my soul knoweth right well."* We were all designed for a purpose, and none of us are here by accident. It is extremely important that we know this truth and hold on to it. There are sadly so many people who feel inadequate, unattractive, and confused about their identity.

2. Authority

Scripture teaches that we ought to submit and respect authority. For many, this is a hard teaching, because to them it seems to indemnify those leaders who may not be just and right in their ways. As believers, we know that God is the one raise up leaders, and because it is He who ultimately puts them in authority, we are to obey them. 1 Peter 2:13-15 states, *"Be subject for the Lord's sake to every human institution, whether it be to the emperor as supreme, or to governors as sent by him to punish those who do evil and to praise those who do good. For this is the will of God, that by doing good you should put to silence the ignorance of foolish people".*

Also, Paul's letter to the Romans, address what our attitude should be towards leadership or governing authority. He says, *"Let everyone be subject to the governing authorities, for there is no authority except that which God has established. The authorities that exist have been established by God. Consequently, whoever rebels against the authority is rebelling against what God has instituted, and those who do so will bring judgment on themselves. For rulers hold no terror for those who do right, but for those who do wrong. Do you want to be free from fear of the one in authority? Then do what is right and you will be commended. For the one in authority is God's servant for your good. But if you do wrong, be afraid, for rulers do not bear the sword for no reason. They are God's servants, agents of wrath to bring punishment on the wrongdoer. Therefore, it is necessary to submit to the authorities, not only because of possible punishment but also as a matter of conscience. This is also why you pay taxes, for the authorities are God's servants, who give their full time to governing. Give to everyone what you owe them: If you owe taxes, pay taxes; if revenue, the revenue; if respect, then respect; if honor, then honor."* Romans 13: 1- 7

Heb. 13:17 calls on us to "Obey them that rule over you, and submit yourselves to their authority: for they keep watch for your souls, as they must give an account, and that they may do it with joy, and not with grief: for that is unprofitable for you."

Figures or symbols of authority include:

- **Family:** Some scriptures that touch on family as a symbol or figure of authority are:

Ephesians 5:21: "Submit to one another out of reverence for Christ."

1 Peter 3:1-7: "Wives, in the same way submit yourselves to your own husbands so that, if any of them do not believe the word, they may be won over without words by the behavior of their wives, when they see the purity and reverence of your lives. Your beauty should not come from outward adornment, such as elaborate hairstyles and the wearing of gold jewelry or fine clothes. Rather, it should be that of your inner self, the unfading beauty of a gentle and quiet spirit, which is of great worth in God's sight. For this is the way the holy women of the past who put their hope in God used to adorn themselves. They submitted themselves to their own husbands, like Sarah, who obeyed Abraham and called him her lord. You are her daughters if you do what is right and do not give way to fear. Husbands, in the same way be considerate as you live with your wives, and treat them with respect as the weaker partner and as heirs with you of the gracious gift of life, so that nothing will hinder your prayers."

1 Peter 5:6: "Humble yourselves, therefore, under God's mighty hand, that he may lift you up in due time."

Deuteronomy 11:19: "You shall teach them to your children, talking of them when you are sitting in your house, and when you are walking by the way, and when you lie down, and when you rise."

Ephesians 6:1-3: "Children, obey your parents in the Lord, for this is right. "Honor your father and mother" (this is the first commandment with a promise), "that it may go well with you and that you may live long in the land."

- **Employer**

Employer: Colossians 4:1 Masters, treat your slaves justly and fairly, knowing that you also have a Master in heaven. Ephesians 6: 5 - 9 *"Slaves, obey your earthly masters with respect and fear, and with sincerity of heart, just as you would obey Christ. Obey them not only to win their favor when their eye is on you, but as slaves of Christ, doing the will of God from your heart. Serve wholeheartedly, as if you were serving the Lord, not people, because you know that the Lord will reward each one for whatever good they do, whether they are slave or free. And masters, treat your slaves in the same way. Do not threaten them, since you know that he who is both their Master and yours is in heaven, and there is no favoritism with him."*

1 Peter 2:16 -19: "Live as free people, but do not use your freedom as a cover-up for evil; live as God's slaves. Show proper respect to everyone, love the family of believers, fear God, honor the emperor. Slaves, in reverent fear of God submit yourselves to your masters, not only to those who are good and considerate, but also to those who are harsh. For it is commendable if someone bears up under the pain of unjust suffering because they are conscious of God."

Ephesians 6:5-7: "Slaves, obey your earthly masters with respect and fear, and with sincerity of heart, just as you would obey Christ. 6 Obey them not only to win their favor when their eye is on you, but as slaves of Christ, doing the will of God from your heart. 7 Serve wholeheartedly, as if you were serving the Lord, not people."

1 Timothy 6:1-3: "All who are under the yoke of slavery should consider their masters worthy of full respect, so that God's name and our teaching may not be slandered. Those who have believing masters should not show

them disrespect just because they are fellow believers. Instead, they should serve them even better because their masters are dear to them as fellow believers and are devoted to the welfare[a] of their slaves. These are the things you are to teach and insist on. If anyone teaches otherwise and does not agree to the sound instruction of our Lord Jesus Christ and to godly teaching."

- **Church**

These following verses speak on the church as a symbol of authority. Hebrews 13:17, *"Obey those who rule over you, and* be submissive, for they watch out for your souls, as those who must give account. Let them do so with joy and not with grief, for that would be unprofitable for you."

1Thes. 5:12-13 "And we urge you, brethren, to recognize those who labor among you, and are over you in the Lord and admonish you and to esteem them very highly in love for their work's sake. Be at peace among yourselves."

1 Timothy 5:17: "The elders who rule well are to be considered worthy of double honor, especially those who work hard at preaching and teaching."

Acts 20:28: "Be on guard for yourselves and for all the flock, among which the Holy Spirit has made you overseers, to shepherd the church of God which He purchased with His own blood."

3. Responsibility

We must give an account to God for our words and deeds. The following verses inform us concerning our accountability.

"So then each of us shall give account of himself to God." Romans 14:12

"But I say to you that for every idle word's man may speak, they will give account of it in the day of judgment." Matt. 12:36

"But if anyone does not provide for his relatives, and especially for members of his household, he has denied the faith and is worse than an unbeliever." 1 Timothy 5:8,

"For by the grace given to me I say to everyone among you not to think of himself more highly than he ought to think, but to think with sober judgment, each according to the measure of faith that God has assigned." Romans 12:3

4. Ownership

Our God is the creator of the universe; everything belongs to Him. Psalm 24:1 clearly reminds us, *"The earth is the Lord's, and all its fullness, the world and those who dwell therein." "Or do you not know that your body is the temple of the Holy Spirit who is in you, whom you have from God, and you are not your own For you were bought at a price; therefore, glorify God in your body and in your spirit, which are God's."* 1Cor 6:19-20, *"Now if you obey me fully and keep my covenant, then out of all nations you will be my treasured possession. Although the whole earth is mine."* Exodus 19:5

Deuteronomy 8:17-18, says, *"You may say to yourself, "My power and the strength of my hands have produced this wealth for me." But remember the Lord your God, for it is he who gives you the ability to produce wealth, and so confirms his covenant, which he swore to your ancestors, as it is today."*

5. Suffering

We will have seasons of suffering. 1 Peter 2:18 -24

"Slaves, in reverent fear of God submit yourselves to your masters, not only to those who are good and considerate, but also to those who are harsh. For it is commendable if someone bears up under the pain of unjust suffering because they are conscious of God. But how is it to your credit if you receive a beating for doing wrong and endure it? But if you suffer for doing good and you endure it, this is commendable before God. To this you were called, because Christ suffered for you, leaving you an example, that you should follow in his steps. "He committed no sin, and no deceit was found in his mouth." When they hurled their insults at him, he did not retaliate; when he suffered, he made no threats. Instead, he entrusted himself to him who judges justly. 24 "He himself bore our sins" in his body on the cross, so that we might die to sins and live for righteousness; "by his wounds you have been healed."

1 Peter 5:10 encourages us thus, " But may the God of all grace, who called us to His eternal glory by Christ Jesus, after you have suffered a while, perfect, establish, strengthen, and settle you."

6. Freedom:

God provides true freedom. John 8:36: "so if the Son sets you free, you will be free indeed."

Galatians 5:13 *"For you were called to freedom, brothers. Only do not use your freedom as an opportunity for the flesh, but through love serve one another."*

1 Peter 2:16-17 *"Live as people who are free, not using your freedom as a cover-up for evil, but living as servants of God. Honor everyone. Love the brotherhood. Fear God. Honor the emperor."*

7. Success:

God brings success. Success is doing and being what God created you to be. Psalm 1:2-3 says, *"but his delight is in the law of the Lord, and in His law he meditates day and night. He shall be like a tree planted by the rivers of water, that brings forth its fruit in its season, whose leaf also shall not wither; and whatever he does shall prosper."*

Joshua 1:8 *This Book of the Law shall not depart from your mouth, but you shall meditate in it day and night, that you may observe to do according to all that is written in it. For then you will make your way prosperous, and then you will have good success.*

Psalm 37:3-4: *"Trust in the Lord and do good; dwell in the land and enjoy safe pasture. Take delight in the Lord and he will give you the desires of your heart."*

1 Kings 2:3: *"and observe what the Lord your God requires: Walk in obedience to him, and keep his decrees and commands, his laws* *and regulations, as written in the Law of Moses. Do this so that you may prosper in all you do and wherever you go."*

This Book of the Law shall not depart from your mouth, but you shall meditate in it day and night, that you may observe to do according to all that is written in it. For then, you will make your way prosperous, and then you will have good success.

Joshua 1:8

CHAPTER 15

THE SHOE – GOSPEL OF PEACE

The Bible says, *"having shod your feet with the preparation of the gospel of peace"*. Let us examine this statement a little closer. Firstly, what is the gospel? The gospel simply means good news - the good news referred to here is salvation through Jesus Christ and the inner peace that it brings. There is a void in the heart of everyone who does not have a relationship with God. There is no one, regardless of wealth, race, achievements, or any other accolades, who are completely satisfied without the presence of God in their lives. It is the presence of God that gives you joy and peace that exceeds human comprehension. It is assuring to know that whatever difficulties, strife and pain life hands to you, there is inner joy and peace that comforts you through it all. The scripture describes this joy as "unspeakable and full of glory in your hearts." It is hard for people who have never experienced this joy to understand how Christians can keep a smile on their faces even when they are in the midst of a crisis.

A new member of my church explained to me why they chose to join our church family. She had heard from a mutual acquaintance that I had lost my son in a vehicular homicide, and like many in our community, she had come around to show her condolences. She visited our church that Sunday, three days after my son had passed, and I stood there and ministered the gospel. My strength and joy considering my present situation demonstrated to her that there was something special in my life and she wanted it in hers. In the same way, my life witnessed to her; you can also quickly tell when somebody is not spiritually grounded. A real relationship with God brings you inner peace. Your relationship with God reminds you that whatever you're going through, you have a God who understands and is able to take care of you. He watches over you and nurtures you. Romans 5:1 Reminds us that "therefore, having been justified by faith, we have peace with God through our Lord Jesus Christ." Peace with God starts with a relationship with Jesus Christ. ("and the peace of God which surpasses all understanding will guard your hearts." Phil 4:7) Not the peace that the world gives, but the peace of God - it surpasses human understanding. The peace of God cannot be explained, but it is crucial that you have this peace during your time of turmoil, which the enemy will attempt to use, hoping to throw you off the path God has predestined for you. Secondly, why are the feet shod with peace? A person's feet are crucial. Imagine if you had no feet; think about what you can't do without your feet. You cannot stand without them; you cannot move without them. You have to depend on something else to move you. You need to have your feet shod because it is your feet that keep you standing, and it's your feet that keep you moving forward. So, when life hands you all kinds of pain, you still need to have the ability to keep standing firm and moving forward.

Shod is a Greek word that means to strap on, or to tie tightly; God wants us to strap on His gospel. He doesn't want us to be flip flop Christians. The problem is that some believers are flip floppers. Why do we wear flip- flops? Perhaps because they are comfortable, but sometimes serving God is neither easy nor comfortable. Some people wear flip-flops because it is easy to slip in and out of them, and many of us treat the gospel like that. We want to slip in and out of our Christianity the same way we slip in and out of our flip- flops. On Sunday morning, you step into your "Christianity" flip flops, and for the rest of the week, you shed the flip flops (Christianity) and put on some other shoes. This is how we treat our faith. We want to have our faith as a matter of convenience, to suite whatever we want to do. So, we leave our relationship with God at home on our date nights or our business transactions. We cannot just slip in and out of faith, jump in today and out tomorrow.

Wherever we go or whatever we do, we are children of God. We must have the gospel of peace strapped on tightly because the moment you take it off the devil is ready to destroy you.

Did you know that you are an evangelist? The Bible says that we should be prepared to share the gospel wherever we are and whenever we can. Learn how to lead someone to a personal relationship with Christ. Every person is called to be prepared with the gospel; 1 Peter 3:15 says, "But in your hearts revere Christ as Lord. Always be prepared to give an answer to everyone who asks you to give the reason for the hope that you have. But do this with gentleness and respect. Do not be a Christian with attitude – share with meekness. You must keep in mind that not everybody is where you are, so steer them to the truth with humility. Just because you know better doesn't mean that they know better. We must have the gospel ready to go. Paul instructed them in 2 Tim 4:2, "Preach the Word; be prepared in season and out of season; correct, rebuke and encourage—with great patience and careful instruction.

CHAPTER 16

THE SHIELD OF FAITH

The shield of faith is another essential element in this armory. The shield of faith is broken down into two areas of faith, namely: Your relationship with God and your relationship with each other.

The Scripture says to take the shield of faith, with which you will be able to quench all the fiery darts of the wicked one. Shields, like many creations of man, has gone through many designs in history. Due to our present depiction or known image of the shield today, it is easy to miss the viewpoint of the writer when he advised us to take up the shield of faith. The shield of faith that the Bible is talking about is the full-body shield. These were tall shields that a warrior could actually stand behind and find full protection. The shield of faith is designed to protect every aspect of your life. So, let us examine this piece of the armor more closely by asking the question: what does it mean to have faith?

Faith

Faith means to rely completely on God - to be confident in Him, to trust Him. You must learn how to trust God in whatever situation you are in. The shield protects your mind and spirit from the many attacks launched by the enemy. The Bible calls these attacks' fiery darts. To better understand this text, you have to realize that historically, in war, the attacker would add flame to their arrows. The intention was to start fires in the camp that would lead to chaos and increased fatality and destruction. It was an intense approach to warfare because it was not just designed to kill the enemy but to wipe out the whole camp. John 10:10 "The thief comes only to steal and kill and destroy." We must be reminded that the enemy is focused on our demise. So, the Word of God says you need to have the shield of faith so that you can quench the fiery darts of the enemy. The enemy throws all kinds of fiery darts against your life; sometimes, it is a word spoken to you or over your life. Words are powerful darts because they can set catastrophic outcomes into motion. Proverbs 18:21 tells us that, "The tongue has the power of life and death, and those who love it will eat its fruit." A bad word spoken over you is worse than someone hitting you in the head with a bat! People can say things to you that start a fire in your heart and burn you so badly you can't sleep for months, if not years.

Fiery darts come in words and even in thoughts; some people have thoughts that throw them off - thoughts of jealousy and distrust. I do believe that the greatest battle plan of the enemy is often subtle. The devil knows that if he plants a seed, he can do more damage, so he sends fiery darts so as to start a fire in your life that will burn and destroy everything around you. One fiery dart that is given an opportunity has the capability to destroy your marriage, your family, friends, valuable relationships, and your entire life as you know it. The Bible says the shield of faith is there to protect us, from the enemy's attempts to ignite these elements in our lives.

We have the Word of God, which reminds us that everything works together for the good of those who love God and are called according to his purpose.

Roman 8:28 And we know that in all things God works for the good of those who love him, who have been called according to his purpose.

The promises of God protect our minds from the lies of the enemy and keep us looking for the good plan God is working out in our lives.

His Word in Matthew 28:20 - "And surely I am with you always, to the very end of the age." - reminds us that He never leaves nor forsakes us, and Psalm 34:19 – "The righteous person may have many troubles, but the Lord delivers him from them all"

These scripture comforts us with His promise of constant protection and covering, in whatever situation we find ourselves. God has it all worked out for us. We can stand on the word and not allow those fiery darts to come in all create madness, chaos, anger, confusion, frustration, jealousy, resentment, depression, and unforgiveness.

Your relationship with God is not exclusive of your relationship with each other, and that is why the Bible tells us that "man cannot say he loves God unless he demonstrates his love for mankind…his neighbor.

This is how we know who the children of God are and who the children of the devil are: Anyone who does not do what is right is not God's child, nor is anyone who does not love their brother and sister". (1 John 3:10,)

"Whoever claims to love God yet hate a brother or sister is a liar. For whoever does not love their brother and sister, whom they have seen, cannot love God, whom they have not seen." Our relationship with God demands that we love people. Jesus tells us even to love our enemies. (1 John 4:20)

Matthew 5:43-48 "You have heard that it was said, 'You shall love your neighbor and hate your enemy.' But I say to you, love your enemies, bless those who curse you, do good to those who hate you, and pray for those who spitefully use you and persecute you, that you may be sons of your Father in heaven; for He makes His sun rise on the evil and on the good, and sends rain on the just and on the unjust. For if you love those who love you, what reward have you? Do not even the tax collectors do the same? And if you greet your brethren only, what do you do more than others? Do not even the tax collectors do so? Therefore, you shall be perfect, just as your Father in heaven is perfect.

You cannot engage in spiritual warfare with hate in your heart, and that's precisely what the devil wants. He wants you to hold grudges, keep malice, and hate people; but, we must love the people who demean and talk nasty about us. We protect ourselves with the love of God. Hatred and unforgiveness will hinders your relationship with God and it weakens your resolve giving the enemy a foothold in your life.

Isaiah 59:2 - But your iniquities have separated between you and your God, and your sins have hid his face from you, that he will not hear.

Ephesians 4:26-27 -- Be ye angry, and sin not: let not the sun go down upon your wrath: Neither give place to the devil.

CHAPTER 17

THE HELMET OF SALVATION

A helmet is designed to cover the head. This is one of the most important element of the armory that God has called us to wear. In the head is where you think and where your intellect lies. The Word of God teaches that "as a man thinketh in his heart so is he" (Proverbs 23:7). Therefore, if your thoughts are not carefully governed, the enemy will come and destroy you.

As a pastor, I have had the opportunity to provide counsel to many persons in difficult times. I have found that most problems are rooted in the individual's thoughts toward their current situation. For example, the difference between a marriage which survive conflicts and one which could not be reconciled, lies in the couple's perspective of forgiveness and self-sacrifice. People suffer from needless worries, depression, phobia, anger, and sickness that originate in their minds. Negative thoughts and emotions that accompany them are so powerful, they can alter or define the projection of one's life. This is what the Bible teaches us in 2 Cor.10:3-5:

'For though we walk in the flesh, we do not war after the flesh:(For the weapons of our warfare are not carnal, but mighty through God to the pulling down of strongholds;)Casting down imaginations, and every high thing that exalteth itself against the knowledge of God, and bringing into captivity every thought to the obedience of Christ;'

The enemy wants you to think that there are intelligence more superior and more intelligent than Jehovah God. Some people get their information from sources that are contradictory to the Word of God, and they believe that these theories presented are factual.

There is no study that can supersede the Word of God. God wants us to protect our thinking and our thought life so that we can cast down those imaginations, reasoning, and false computations. If we do not address and demolish these false and misleading messages, then the enemy will be able to confuse and distort our thinking. I remember my first few classes in school where Darwinism was taught. I had never heard of this alternative to God's creation as presented by the bible. His presentation with the progression of humanity from monkeys seemed so plausible to my childish imagination.

What they did not tell us in class was that this was not real science, but just Charles Darwin's imagination. I am glad I was able to see it for what it really was just theory with no proof and biblical contractions. Millions miss out on a relationship with God due to this false thesis.

Whatever we think is how we will live; we cannot live correctly if we don't think correctly. Therefore, we are instructed to cast down imagination, and every high thing that exalts itself against the knowledge of God. We must subject our thoughts to the Word of God, bringing every thought into captivity, and make it obedient to Christ. There is a crisis in this information allowing every viewpoint, regardless of how absurd, gets heard. These demonically driven misinformation's are made available to the innocent young minds who do not have enough understanding to filter out what is good or bad. People are deceived by so-called 'men of God.' False teachers are everywhere clothed in charm and charisma, often empowered by sorcery.

The Word of God is the standard manual for human wellbeing. You have to learn how to evaluate the valueless information you read online, or information perpetrated through school systems that aims to change the world from what God intended it to be. We have to put on the helmet of salvation because we have to protect our thoughts and minds. We cannot allow any and everything in if we're going to be victorious in our Christian walk. *Philippians 4:8 8 Finally, brethren, whatsoever things are true, whatsoever things are honest, whatsoever things are just, whatsoever things are pure, whatsoever things are lovely, whatsoever things are of good report; if there be any virtue, and if there be any praise, think on these things.* The Word of God is very clear on what should occupy the mind of a Christian.

It seems like negative news, false information move around the internet more quickly than anything that is worthy and life-giving. We have to be careful not to become a part of this demonic attitude. If you don't have anything good or encouraging to say about someone, you should seriously consider not saying anything at all, unless it is with the intent of helping to correct or edify. I have seen so many instances where ministries and persons are seriously maimed by the careless dissemination of misleading information. Keep in mind that everyone has something that they would rather not place on a billboard. It doesn't matter how well put together you are on the outside; on the inside, there are inner battles that we regularly fight. Since you have things in your life that you would rather address in private, then it would be a good thing not to be quick to publicize every negative thing you hear about a brother or sister. The Bible teaches us to be free of evil speaking and gossiping. To this end, we must hold each other accountable. It is our responsibility to stop gossip by calling it out and disengaging from any participation in such activity.

Psalm 19:14 - Let the words of my mouth, and the meditation of my heart, be acceptable in thy sight, O Lord, my strength, and my redeemer.

Our job is to pick up each person when they fall and keep moving. Let the strong carry the weak. There are days when we feel weak and vulnerable and really need the love, care, and encouragement of our brothers and sisters.

2 Corinthians 10:5 - We demolish arguments and every pretension that sets itself up against the knowledge of God, and we take captive every thought to make it obedient to Christ.

Put on the helmet to protect your thinking, for out of your mind and heart flows the issues of life. Do not allow anyone to take away your joy, and do not take anybody else's joy either. The enemy wants to destroy you and to use you to harm others as well. But we should walk in the light, being fully aware of his devices. Greater is He that is in us than he that is in the world. We have a responsibility to live according to the Word of God and not according to the media outlets and celebrities.

Start every day with the decision to put on the whole armor of God. Do not be flip-flop Christians! We should be Christians all the time. Not just on Sundays, but every day.

CHAPTER 18

SWORD OF THE SPIRIT

The sword of the Spirit is the Word of God. We need to know what the Word of God says about every situation in life. Psalm 119:16 says I will delight myself in thy statutes: I will not forget thy word.

The Bible addresses all aspects of life directly or indirectly. Psalm 119 :1 say "Your Word have I hid in my heart that I might not sin against you. I should make decisions based on the Word of God. I must be rooted and grounded in the Word of God. The enemy wants us to believe that what we see on television and the internet and what celebrities say supersedes God's Word. In doing so, we have subconsciously elevated man's intellect over the intellect of God. In this informational and technological age, we can be conned by the devil into thinking that we have an answer and explanation for everything. We seem to be smarter, with more opportunities to be educated, yet it seems like the more information we have, the more we move away from the wisdom of God. (Romans 1:22, Professing themselves to be wise, they became fools.)

God is the only one who knows everything. He is the creator of all things, and he gives us a manual for life – His Word in the Bible. It does matter what we do or how we do. If we do something that is contrary to God's instruction, it will eventually lead to an ineffective or destructive end. Regardless of what the so-called experts and researchers say, we simply can't go against the Word of God and expect it to end well. I remember when my wife and I moved into our first home, we were so excited and went out to get an entertainment center. After picking out the one we liked, we were given a ticket to pick it up. The item was delivered to me in a box. Being rather new and naïve to American life - after all, the craft men in my native land of Jamaica would have delivered the unit completely ready to use. I told the delivery man that the item he delivered to me was someone else's order. He took my receipt and gave me the shocking news. "This is your order, sir; you have to go home and put it together." I took it home and anxiously began to put the pieces together; after all, I am very handy. Without consulting the manual, I proceeded to put it together, and it was beginning to take shape.

After two hours, it was time to put some final parts in, and it was impossible to do. How could this be? I thought. I soon realized that I had assembled the pieces out of order because I did not consult with the manual. Needless to say, I had to take it apart and start all over again. Life is like that box that was delivered to me. It was well thought out, and everything was put there by the manufacturer, God, who created us and gave us life and purpose. If we are to properly put it together, we need the guidance of His Word. If we allow it, life would be a beautiful work of art, fulfilling our intended purpose. Yet, like I did that evening, most people do not like to read the manual for life; we just start assembling parts, acting like we know how until we get stuck, realizing that we have been doing it wrong all along. We then spend many seasons in our lives rebuilding for bad decisions along the way. Unfortunately, many just start the same process over and over again. Remember, God created us with intricate detail; we cannot pretend we know more than the manufacturer. We have to take the time to find out how and when to make the next move. So why not follow the "manual"? We need the Word of God - the Bible. *With what can a young man cleanse his way? By taking heed thereto according to thy word. Psalm 119:9.*

CHAPTER 19

GOD SPEAKS

The Word of God holds great importance in the life of the Christian. It would be very remiss of me not to spend a little more time on this subject. Since it is the manual for life, an even deeper understanding can be useful in not missing out on what God may want to say to you.

"The fear of the Lord is the beginning of knowledge: but fools despise wisdom and instruction

Proverbs 1:7."

The logos

Logos is the written Word of God. God's word is living and is sharp and powerful. Hebrews 4:12, For the Word of God, is quick, and powerful, and sharper than any two-edged sword, piercing even to the dividing asunder of soul and spirit, and of the joints and marrow, and is a discerner of the thoughts and intents of the heart. The written Word of God is crucial to a Christian's victory. You will remember that when Jesus was tempted by Satan, He responded with the logos, (Matt 4:1-3).

Then Jesus was led by the Spirit into the wilderness to be tempted by the devil. 2 After fasting forty days and forty nights, he was hungry. 3 The tempter came to him and said, "If you are the Son of God, tell these stones to become bread." 4 Jesus answered, "It is written: 'Man shall not live on bread alone, but on every word that comes from the mouth of God.' Paul instructed Timothy to study the logo 2 Timothy 2:15. Be diligent to present yourself approved to God, a worker who does not need to be ashamed, rightly dividing the word of truth.

The Psalmist says, "Your word I have hidden in my heart, That I might not sin against You."

(Psalm 119:11)

Let not mercy and truth forsake you; Bind them around your neck, write them on the tablet of your heart,

Proverbs 3:3

Every believer should make it a habit of reading, meditating, and memorizing the logos.

Rhema Word

Rhema word is God's Word revealed by the Holy Spirit at a specific time to help you address a specific need. The Spirit of

God can take a verse or Scripture that you have read several times before, but on this occasion, God gives you a fresh revelation that addresses your present situation. This revelation makes your heart come alive, and offer the light you need to propel your life into a impactful decision. This is the Rhema word of God. It is a word for the moment, a word for 'right now.'

CHAPTER 20

PRAYER

The verse (Ephesians 6:18) closes this way, saying: "Praying always with all prayer and supplication in the Spirit, and watching thereunto with all perseverance and supplication for all saints;"

Prayer is the real work. It is the divine spiritual tool that God has given to us, so that we can operate on the earth and have heavenly impact. This is the reason why the Bible says "pray always". We need to understand that prayer has an intrinsic value. Jesus spent all night praying, seeking God. He set the example for us and demonstrated the power of prayer. Jesus showed us the importance of prayer, yet most of us live our lives without prayer or barely praying. Even so when we do pray, we pray like it's a snap-chat, always on the fly. We do not take the time to get down on our knees before God and wait in his presence, not just asking him for direction but also waiting for an answer.

The disciples were enamored by Jesus's authority; they observed that he would get up spend several hours in the morning to pray then demons and sickness responded immediately to his command. So much so that disciples requested of Jesus, "Please teach how to pray," (Luke 11:1).

Jesus spoke about the power of prayer and the heavenly response that is available when we pray in Matthew 26:53 *"Thinkest thou that I cannot now pray to my Father, and he shall presently give me more than twelve legions of angels?"* How can we ignore one of the most powerful tools in life by our disregard for prayer and expect to win the victory over satan? Satan's powerful strategy is to have us start our days with our telephones and social media instead of prayer. We also have Daniel in the scripture, who prayed –the Bible says he prayed three times per day; some of us pray three times a day only over our meals. Jesus commanded us to pray when he said *"that men always ought to pray, and not lose heart"* (Luke 18:1), and Paul also echoes the same thought in 1Thes 5:17, saying, *"pray without ceasing."* Prayer is very important.

You cannot live a successful Christian life without an active prayer life. Our victory over the flesh and the devil will require God's strength. Prayer is the key to your spiritual survival.

The posture of prayer

The Bible says that we should pray always. This is "the posture of prayer." Some people pray only when they're going through some form of hardship. Prayer for them is a last resort. They turn to God when there is bad news, with no one else to turn to. This is not an indictment against people who only pray in times of trouble, but we have been instructed to stay in a posture of prayer. Our posture towards prayer must be one that causes us to come before Him continually recognizing Him as Lord over our lives.

The word prayer has two elements: Firstly praying means to worship. When we come before God in prayer we must include worship. The Bible says we come into His gates with thanksgiving and into His courts with praise.

Worshipping God is of utmost importance. Your life was created for His glory so you must never cease from giving worship to Him. Your first and most important duty is to worship God. Staying in the attitude of worship invites the presence of God in your life and situation. We must persevere in worship even times of trouble, pain, heartbreak, or sickness. There is probably nothing more disheartening to the devil than a child of God praising and worshipping Almighty God in their darkest moment. Job said, *"Though He slays me, yet will I trust Him. Even so, I will defend my own ways before Him."* (Job 13:15) Let your heart echo this sentiment, that regardless of what I am going through, I will still worship; I shall give Him praise. I have decided that no matter what the enemy throws at me, I'm going to stay in the posture of prayer and the attitude of worship. Psalm 100:4 says, *"Enter into His gates with thanksgiving, And into His courts with praise. Be thankful to Him and bless His name."* There's something about worshiping and praising God that gives your heart peace and joy. It lifts your spirit into the presence of God. Don't wait until it is convenient; don't wait until trouble comes to be in the posture of prayer "pray always."

Secondly, prayer also means to direct your requests to God. This is, taking your needs, troubles or request to Him. An old hymn says, "oh what grief we often forfeit oh what needless pain we bear, all because do not carry everything to God in prayer." Prayer speaks to our faith because it says to us that I know that God can handle whatever I am dealing with. I know that God can supply all my needs. I recognized God as my source, to see Him as my helper and healer. I always look to him. "I will look to the hills from whence cometh my help, my help cometh from the Lord who created the heaven and the earth." (Psalm 121:1).

We pray always fixing our gaze on God.

Never be too proud to call out to God. You have to learn to come before God, knowing that you have a big God that wants to hear from you. He knows what you need, but He is waiting for you to reach out and claim it. I love the story of the woman with the issue of blood (Mark 5:25-34). She didn't care about who was in the crowd; she didn't care what people would say about her or what they thought of her. She just knew that if she could just touch the hem of his garment, she would be made whole. She had tried other sources for help to no avail. She realized that she needed God to heal her body.

He gives you permission in Matthew 11:28, "Come to Me, all you who labor and are heavy laden, and I will give you rest." He says, come onto me boldly, come to the throne of heaven – "Let us, therefore, come boldly to the throne of grace that we may obtain mercy and find grace to help in time of need." (Hebrew 4:16). He invites us to bring our petition to Jesus. He wants to hear from you.

Come and make your supplication before Him, praying in the spirit. In other words, do not pray according to your flesh but according to the spirit. The problem is that some of us only pray according to our flesh, calling on God only for our lustful desires. We don't take time to find out what is God's perfect will before we pray. For example you may decide to go into a relationship that we know God does not approve of, and then we ask God to fix it. We proceed with the relationship base on our external biases. If the man is tall, dark, and handsome, or she is curvy and charming and has met our physical requirement, that's all that matters in the initiation period.

Then when the devil shows up in the relationship, we pray for God to make it work for us. We would do well to read the story of Samson in the book of Judges - external beauty is not God's standard. Yes, Delilah was beautiful but God had someone else for Samson. His choice was his demise because he took a wife from a foreign nation when God clearly says he should not. God cannot bless what he has not permitted. If we are not careful, we will forfeit getting results to our prayer because we come to God with a fleshly driven prayer. If we want to have power and favor, we must learn how to pray according to the spirit of God; we must allow the spirit of God to guide our prayer life. Rom 8:26 Likewise, the Spirit also helps in our weaknesses. For we do not know what we should pray for as we ought, but the Spirit Himself makes intercession for us with groanings which cannot be uttered.

He also told us to be watchful and prudent! Here's the problem, some people pray without expectancy. When you pray, and you do not expect anything, then all you did was engage in an exercise. Don't come to God with trouble and then leave with it, don't come with your sicknesses and leave with them, rather come with a heart of expectation. When you go to God, you have to know and believe that He is well able to do what you ask of Him. He is a father who cares about your situation. He will not give you a stone when you ask for bread (Luke 11:11-13). We need to expect that when we pray God will answer. He's will not give you sickness when you are in need of healing, neither will He's give you pain for joy. God will turn your sorrows into dancing. That's the God you serve! When you go to him, be expectant that He will do what you ask Him to do. He will turn your life around, fix the family issues, provide new financial opportunities and blesses your investments. When you go to God, know that He hears, and He will answer you. After you have spent time on your knees with Him, walk out of the room, saying, *"God, I'm ready for the connections, I'm ready for you to take me to the next level, Lord I'm ready for the things I've been asking you for. I'm ready for my blessing.* Order my steps." After you have done that walk around with an attitude of gratitude, knowing that any day or any time now, the things that you have asked God for will be released in your life. He said, be watchful in your prayer!

Psalm 28:7 says, The Lord is my strength and my shield; my heart trusted in him, and I am helped: therefore, my heart greatly rejoiceth; and with my song will I praise him.

Posture also means that we have to be spiritually, mentally, and emotionally in the right place with God. The Bible says, "If we regard iniquity in our heart, God will not hear us" (Psalm 66:18). So, when we go to God in prayer, it requires that we address our relationship with God and others. He wants to remind us that there are things in our life that need to be addressed. We must have the right attitude of heart when we pray. Come humble and broken before God. The right posture doesn't mean on your knees like some mistakenly think. For some it could be while you are driving along the road and praying (don't close your eyes). You can be cleaning your house and praying. You could be at your work, with your crazy boss or co-worker driving you nuts, and you can still be praying. Prayer will keep the devil away. So, the next time your spouse, your boss, or any other person attacks you, just begin to pray and call on the name of Jesus Christ of Nazareth and put the enemy to flight. Stay in a posture of prayer.

Perseverance

To pray with perseverance means to pray regardless of what continues to happen in your life. When Jesus was tempted by the devil, he had more than one encounter with him. I would like to make it clear for you to understand that there will be many series of encounters that you will experience with the devil on the way to your victory. The Bible says that Jesus was tempted for a season and He overcome that temptation (Luke 4:13, And when the devil had ended all the temptation, he departed from him for a season). This is the way the devil works. There are times when he will attack you intensely; thus, you will have to learn how not to become overwhelmed by your situation. Develop the attitude of Job, which says, I heard what the news says, about what's happened, all my sons are dead, and my livestock is gone, but regardless of those reports I still have confident in God. I will still give Him praise. Who can I turn to if not God? Job says, "Even if he slays me, I'm still going to give him praise, even if he inflicts my body" (Job 13:15). Would you say, 'I will praise God, even if the doctor's report is not favorable?' Would you still praise Him, even if cancer rocks your body? Have you made the decision that whatever comes your way you will maintain an attitude of perseverance? Be confident that whatever God does is well done. The Bible tells us in John 11 that Lazarus died after being sick. Jesus was summoned, but he didn't show up until four days after he had passed away. Martha and Mary were disturbed that Jesus had arrived too late to help their brother.

I believe that there are many people who feel that way when faced with difficulties. It often seems like our prayers are falling on deaf ears. However, even though Lazarus had died, for Jesus, it didn't mean it was over, for he is the resurrection and the life.

As a child of God you cannot allow yourself to lose hope, because the enemy will use it as an opportunity to creep into your life. I know people who have turned to witchcraft because they were not willing to wait on the Lord. I have seen women enter into ungodly relationships because of financial reasons. I am writing this book to encourage someone today, do not lose hope, do not give up on your prayer life, do not stop persevering. Be strong and encouraged yourself with the word of God. When Jesus shows up, even though the situation may look like it is dead, He is still on time. Persevere in prayer!

Pray for others

Pray for other people; he said always pray for the saints. The Bible says *the effective, fervent prayer of a righteous man avails much. (James 5:16)* Your prayer has power!

The problem is that we spend most of our time praying for ourselves. But there's something incredible that God has called us to do. He said we should pray one for another and to lift up each other. The truth is that from time to time we too are desperately in need of others to pray with and for us. Take the opportunity to stand in the gap for somebody today. United prayer is power in the spiritual realm. The scripture says "One will chase a thousand but two will chase ten thousand." This is how we triumph over the devil. I praying for somebody, and somebody praying for me and together we come into agreement.

"One can chase a thousand, but two can put chase ten thousand to flight" (Deuteronomy 32:30).

Are you willing to do battle for somebody?

CHAPTER 21

THE DESTINY OF DEMONS

Now let me give you some good news. The destiny of every demon assigned to your life has already been decided. When

Jesus encountered a demon-possessed man during his earthly ministry, the demons asked, "Have you come here to torment us before the time?" (Matt. 8:29). Demons understand something about their eternal destiny. The phrase "before the time" could mean that they feared premature expulsion from the man, but it probably meant premature judgment to hell. The destiny of demons can be summarized in three phases of confinement.

Present Confinement

Some demons are currently confined. John described the release of some of these demons in Revelation 9 during the Great Tribulation when they will come from the bottomless pit to afflict the people. Jude identified another group of demons whom God *"has kept in eternal chains under gloomy darkness until the judgment of the great day"* (Jude 6). Apparently, the crime of these fallen angels were so horrendous that they would never again experience any degree of liberty (2 Pet. 2:4).

Millennial Confinement

During the Great Tribulation, there *"are demonic spirits, performing signs, who go abroad to the kings of the whole world, to assemble them for battle on the great day of God the Almighty."* (Rev. 16:14). As demons are in part responsible for the battle of Armageddon, it is reasonable to expect they would be prevented from making war during the millennial reign of Christ.

While their millennial destiny is not specifically identified in the Bible, most commentators would agree that they would be confined with Satan, their leader, in the bottomless pit (Rev. 20:3). They certainly are not active during Christ's reign on the earth.

Eternal Confinement

One of the key thoughts to keep in mind when attempting to understand hell is to remember it was never the will of God that anyone should go there (1 Pet. 3:9). When confronted with that truth, the obvious question is, *"Why did God created hell in the first place?"* The answer to that question is found in Matthew 25:41. Hell was "prepared for the devil and his angels." A man will only go to hell by choice, his choice as expressed by his rejection of Christ. Demons are apparently aware that someday they will be eternally confined to the lake of fire (Matt. 8:29).

Christians Become Judges

The Bible also teaches that angels are not exempt from judgment. Paul asked the Corinthians, "Do you not know that we are to judge angels?" (1 Cor. 6:3). Toward the end of the age, it will be our responsibility as Christians to represent God in the role of judge. It may be that during the Tribulation, the millennial kingdom, or eternity to follow, we will serve as judges similar to the judges who ruled before Israel's first king. As judges, we will be given a position of authority over angels.

CHAPTER 22

GO IN CONFIDENCE

Let me, in closing, put this in perspective for you. Remember that we became acquainted with the power of darkness (the devil) and light (Jehovah God), and we were given a front-row seat as God overcame the attempt of the devil to exalt himself. Throughout the history of mankind, we have seen the enemy throw some powerful blows, but the all-powerful God has always responded and overcame. The ultimate blow was the fall of humanity which threw this world into sin and the disarray we now see around us, but as always, God our heavenly Father answered with the Messiah Jesus Christ, the savior of the world.

Jesus descended from heaven and was carefully delivered to the womb of the Virgin Mary through a process in which he took on humanity. The battle was on in the devil's territory. The devil tried to stop it through the assassination of thousands of newborns, but God, the father, overcame that plan too. Again, in the desert, he tried to get Jesus to forget about the mission with the offer of great fame, wealth, and prestige, but Jesus stayed focused. I can't help but wonder as I reflect now how many have lost focus of their life's mission in search of wealth, fame, and earthly comfort. Facing the reality of the suffering ahead, I believe the enemy was present in the garden of Gethsemane trying to convince Jesus to give up the assignment of dying for humanity, but yet again that battle was won when these words shocked the almost silent garden "Not my will Lord, but Yours be done!'

Jesus was crucified on a Roman cross and was buried. How Satan must have laughed! Finally, He is dead and buried! However, the sigh of relief would be short-lived as Jesus rose from the dead with all power in his hand. Matthew 28:18, "And Jesus came and spoke to them, saying, "All authority has been given to Me in heaven and on earth."

This series of events is very important for every born-again Christian to understand. Let me highlight a few passages that will help you understand the defeat which landed on the enemy and the victory handed to Christians since Satan played into the master plan of God. The crucifixion of Jesus Christ was necessary for the empowerment of the great army of God to be released in the earth. Let us read the following verses and meditate on all that God has done for us and the position he has given to us to defeat the enemy every day!

Another parable He put forth to them, saying: "The kingdom of heaven is like a mustard seed, which a man took and sowed in his field, 32 which indeed is the least of all the seeds; but when it is grown it is greater than the herbs and becomes a tree so that the birds of the air come and nest in its branches."

Matthew 13:31-32

Most assuredly, I say to you, unless a grain of wheat falls into the ground and dies, it remains alone; but if it dies, it produces much grain.

John 12:24

Inasmuch then as the children have partaken of flesh and blood, He Himself likewise shared in the same, that through death He might destroy him who had the power of death, that is, the devil,

Hebrews 2:14

But if I do, though you do not believe Me, believe the works, that you may know and believe that the Father is in Me, and I in Him.

John 10:38

But the Helper, the Holy Spirit, whom the Father will send in My name, He will teach you all things, and bring to your remembrance all things that I said to you.

John 14:26

Nevertheless, I tell you the truth. It is to your advantage that I go away; for if I do not go away, the Helper will not come to you; but if I depart, I will send Him to you.

John 16:7

This Jesus hath God raised up, whereof we all are witnesses.

Acts 2:32

But if the Spirit of Him who raised Jesus from the dead dwells in you, He who raised Christ from the dead will also give life to your mortal bodies through His Spirit who dwells in you.

Romans 8:11

And what is the exceeding greatness of His power toward us who believe, according to the working of His mighty power, which He worked in Christ when He raised Him from the dead and seated Him at His right hand in the heavenly places, far above all principality and power and might and dominion, and every name that is named, not only in this age but also in that which is to come. And He put all things under His feet and gave Him to be head over all things to the church, which is His body, the fullness of Him who fills all in all.

Ephesians 1:19-23

And raised us up together, and made us sit together in the heavenly places in Christ Jesus.

Ephesians 2:6

So, Jesus said to them again, "Peace to you! As the Father has sent Me, I also send you."

John 20:21

Use the following pages to reflect on your faith journey.

- Have you knowingly or unknowingly allowed the devil in your life?

- Are you able to stand firm in the midst of trials and all other challenges the devil throws at you?

- How are you engaging your full armor in the battle against the enemy?

I hope this book Unmasking Darkness enlightens your mind encourage your heart and assure you that you are more than a conqueror through Christ Jesus our lord. Go in confidence!

- Dr. Stephen R. Buchanan

www.ingramcontent.com/pod-product-compliance
Lightning Source LLC
Chambersburg PA
CBHW072202100526
44589CB00015B/2335